Tell Me When You're Going to Die

and

*I'll Tell You
How Well You Can Afford to Live*

The Top 10 Retirement Secrets Wall Street Doesn't Want You to Know

By

Stephen J. Kelley, CSA

© Copyright 2015

Safety First Financial Planners
33 Main Street, Suite 201
Nashua, NH 03064

844-4-FREE-MO

www.FreeMoneyGuys.com

"Free Money Guy®" Stephen Kelley can be heard, along with his co-host Mark Perkins, on the Free Money Radio Hour at 9:00 a.m. every Tuesday and Wednesday morning on 1590 AM WSMN in Nashua, and Sundays at Noon on 980 WCAP in Lowell.

Additionally, Steve is heard weekly on the nationally syndicated "America Tonight" with Kate Delaney.

As well as "Tell Me When You're Going to Die," Steve is author of the books, "Safe Harbors That Can Reduce Taxes, Remove Risk and Protect Your Retirement," and "Retirement Planning Riches," both available on Amazon.com, FreeMoneyGuys.com, and selected fine bookstores..

Through his books, radio shows, newspaper columns, college workshops, and financial planning practice, Steve has help thousands of Boomers and retirees gain a stronger financial footing and build dependable, steadfast and unfailing retirement plans.

Steve lives with this wife Mary and the two youngest of his amazing kids in Nashua, NH.

His financial planning practice, Safety First Financial Planners is located at 33 Main Street in Nashua. He can be reached at 603-881-8811, or online at www.FreeMoneyGuys.com.

Contents

Author's note 1

Introduction: Tell Me When You're Going to Die 4
    Old Age and the Decline in Financial Literacy 7

About Fiduciaries (Maybe the #1 Secret Wall Street Hopes You Don't Find Out!) 12
    Lessons from the street 18

Big Secret #10: 401(k)s were not done for you, they were done to you 23
    Bob, Alice, Ted and Carol 31

Big Secret #9: Tax deferral is often a tax trap 35

Big Secret #8: Gravity cannot be ignored 40

Big Secret #7: Wall Street counts on your complacency. 47

Big Secret #6: Wall Street hasn't a clue what to do. 50

Big Secret #5: Most investors get much less than the market average. 60

Big Secret #4: Average rates of return lie 64
    Removing risk is much more important than increasing gains. 65

Big Secret #3: Bonds are not a safe alternative. 69

Big Secret #2: The only guarantees on variable annuities are the fees you will pay 74

Big Secret #1: The very best thing for income planning is annuities 83

    What Makes Them So Good? 85

    Wall Street hates this part 93

    These Are Not Your Father's Annuities... 96

    Protection from Stock Market Losses.. 100

    The Big Lie.. 101

Receive lifetime income without giving up control of your money 108

    Long life vs. Good life... 108

Last Things First: The key to successful income planning............... 113

    Lessons from the street 119

How Safe is "Safe"?.. 125

    Variations on a theme.. 133

The 10 Most Common Objections to Annuities 138

Index... 148

"Truth is the daughter of time, not of authority."
— Francis Bacon

Author's note

As I sit down to write what is my fourth book, I wonder, as I always do, what will be produced at the end of this process. I typically don't really start with outlines; usually I put together a bunch of newspaper columns I've written, or pick up some white papers and put them together, or sometimes just record what's on my mind. To clear up any confusion, or lest you think I missed it, it should be noted that some of the material and memes in this book can be found in others that I have written, and in my weekly newspaper columns. As I am not in this to sell books, but to help people retire abundantly, I make no apologies; any repetitious material herein bears repeating.

The key, I guess, is just to start writing, as I am doing now. I don't know if this paragraph will end up in the book, or where it will end up if it does; suffice it to say that it's the first paragraph I wrote and we'll see if it's included (as you can see, it was!).

Why do I bring this up? Because as I am writing this it occurs to me that this is much the same way people do their financial and income planning (two different things, by the way). More often than not, people do a little something here…perhaps open an IRA; a little more there…like maybe fund a 401(k); follow some ad hoc advice…like maybe open a Roth IRA; purchase a product or two…like maybe a variable annuity or even a life insurance policy, and in the end have no idea what they should do with it or why. Does this sound familiar to you?

Now, while it may very well work fine as a creative process, I can tell you categorically it's a terrible way to craft a plan to determine your future financial viability. There you need to be focused and intentional. You need to understand why you are doing what you are doing, you need to define and focus what kind of outcome you want and work backwards, and you must, always, without exception, have a complete and accurate understanding of everything you do and every component of your plan. Otherwise, you are destined to fail.

Hopefully this book will provide some insight into how to approach these issues and the types of questions you should be asking yourself, and ultimately, answering for yourself.

Before you begin, however, I have to cover my back side, so here it is: Nothing in this book is intended as, nor should be construed to be advice of any kind: financial, accounting, legal or otherwise. Before acting on any of the information contained herein you should consult with your own professional advisor in this area. Nothing in this book should be construed to be true unless you have personally validated it. Everything in this book is purely the opinion of the author unless attributed to another source, in which case the cited source is assumed to be true and accurate. In no way is the author responsible for inaccuracies of cited studies or sources.

So, all that being said, and having appropriately covered my backside should you have the crazy whim of actually believing anything I have recorded here, let's dig in!

"Truth will always be truth, regardless of lack of understanding, disbelief or ignorance." — W. Clement Stone

Introduction: Tell Me When You're Going to Die

Whoa…are you kidding me? What kind of a title is that? Are you trying to stir up some kind of trouble? Or just be controversial?

Really, I've heard it all since I started asking that question. Sometimes people get really angry. Others are somewhat confused, and wonder what I'm getting at. Others seem to understand right away and nod and smile. Others don't ever get it. But I can tell you the question is real. It has a purpose. And it's perhaps the most important question that needs to be asked and answered when we are starting the retirement income planning process.

In fact, it's the thing that stumps most financial planners and is the reason so many plans are poorly designed, and it's all because we really don't know, unless you are one of the unfortunate few who is afflicted with a life threatening or mortal disease. As I write that, it occurs to me that it's presumptuous of me to assign a value judgement. Perhaps you don't regard your situation as unfortunate or as an affliction, so while not really wanting to retract it, and as I feel it needs to be addressed, let me say I leave it up to you to determine how it will impact your life.

That all being said, the bottom line is that unless you are in that category you have no idea at all how long you are going to walk this Earth. You may have seen the Time Magazine cover from this past February (2015) which featured a photo of a baby with the headline: "This Baby Could Live to Be 142 Years Old." The one thing we do know is that people are living longer and longer lifespans. It's not uncommon in this day and age for a retirement to be nearly as long as a career was…sometimes as long as several decades. With that kind of potential unemployment span in front of you, it's really important to get your retirement choices correct, right? Right? So don't you think it's time you really started thinking seriously about it?

My industry certainly has. Beginning January 2016, all newly issued life insurance contracts and annuities will have to reserve to age 120. While this makes policy holders much more secure in some ways, it is changing the face of this industry in other ways.

The unfortunate thing about this is that most people don't consider this most important question. Here are what I consider to be some really alarming statistics.[1]

- Seventy eight percent of middle-class Americans don't have a financial adviser or plan.
- Forty percent of people 45 to 54 rely on friends and family for their financial advice.
- Only 18% of pre-retirees who work with advisers have written retirement plans.
- Only 25% of respondents 45 to 54 who receive (professional) financial advice act on it.
- Only 50% have a will, and fewer still, 42%, have a living will or health care proxy.
- Sixty percent of people fear running out of money more than they fear death.
- Eighty one percent of Americans are worried that they won't have enough money for retirement.
- The average 401(k) fund balance ages 65-74: $148,900.
- The average 401(k) runs out in around six years.

---

[1] "The Future of Retirement: A Balancing Act." 2015. Accessed May 9, 2015. http://www.hsbc.com/~/media/HSBC-com/about-hsbc/structure-and-network/retirement/global-reports/150119-en-global.pdf.

- Those with financial plans accumulated nearly 250% more retirement savings than those without a financial plan in place.
- Approximately $270,000 is missing from the average retirement plan, primarily due to poor or absent planning.

I could go on and on. But the bottom line is most Baby Boomers are woefully unprepared for retirement. If you don't believe me, ask yourself, "Is $148,900 enough to build a 20 to 30 year retirement on?"

Old Age and the Decline in Financial Literacy

Consistent with prior studies of cognitive decline in old age, we find that financial literacy scores decline by about one percentage point each year after age 60. We test for possible cohort effects and find that the rate of decline in financial literacy is nearly identical among men, stockowners, older, and college-educated respondents. Confidence in financial decision making abilities does not decline with age….A separate analysis using data that include measures of cognitive ability and financial literacy suggest that a natural decline in both fluid and crystallized intelligence in

> old age contributes to falling financial literacy scores…[2]

In a nutshell, the result of this study is that as we get older we lose our ability to make wise financial decisions, but our confidence in ourselves goes up. This is a deadly combination. Especially if we are flying solo.

Food for Thought:

- Do you have an income retirement plan?
- Have you employed the services of an income retirement planner?
- Why or why not?

Before going on, let me say I get it. I understand why most people don't have professional financial help. The fact is, you don't trust us. And with good reason. There is so much noise and so many conflicting opinions. Everybody, it seems wants only one thing—to separate you from your money. Billions of dollars are spent every year in lobbying Congress and silly advertisements about blue dots, orange numbers and green lines. And everyone seems to win except for us.

---

[2] Finke, Michael S. and Howe, John S. and Huston, Sandra J., Old Age and the Decline in Financial Literacy (August 24, 2011). Forthcoming in Management Science. Available at SSRN: http://ssrn.com/abstract=1948627 or http://dx.doi.org/10.2139/ssrn.1948627

Let me address that for a moment, because it really is how I came with this whole idea for a book. It was several years ago in an ABC Financial Planning course I was teaching at a local college. We were discussing how much you need to have set aside for retirement, and I ran for the class that silly ING commercial with people running around carrying big orange numbers.

It was the one with the guy trimming the hedge, the one that starts out with, "Hey Clark, what's that?" Then "Clark" goes on to explain how it's his number and what he's determined he is going to need in order to retire. And then he asks the hedge trimmer what his number is and he responds that it's a "bazillion, gazillion."

At any rate, I always sided with the hedge trimmer on this one. As I was explaining this to the class, someone asked me why. My response was, well, how can this guy possibly know what his number is if he doesn't know how long he has to plan for? In other words, tell me when you are going to die and I can create a plan for you. Otherwise it's all pie in the sky. Right?

Anyway, that took off, and as time went on, when people would ask how much I thought they needed, I would ask them, when are you going to die? I did this partly as shock value, and also because it brings home, very quickly, what the key issues are with regard to retirement planning…unless you know how long the plan is for, you cannot possibly know how much you need.

We know some things about this. One thing we know is people trying to do it alone don't very often get it right. Of those doing it on their own, about 40% estimate too short a life, and run out of money during retirement. About 40% guess too long a life, and end up with way too much at the end. While some might not regard that as being as serious as running out, in my mind it's just as bad. What it means is, most of the time, you've cheated yourself out of the best life you can have for fear that you will live longer than you actually lived. I regard this as tragic. Only about 20% actually get it right, and for most of them it's pure luck.

Much of the material in this book emerges from this one issue. Most of the challenges with regard to retirement income planning have to do with the uncertainty of lifespan and the fact that many of us are going to need income for up to 30 years, or even more. Market risk, inflation, low interest rates, taxes, long-term healthcare, and many other retirement issues are either caused by, or exacerbated by lengthy and uncertain lifespans.

One thing is for sure, it's very complex, and the price for getting it wrong can be very, very high. In addition, with the disappearance of pensions, the emergence of defined-contribution plans, the changes and uncertainty surrounding Social Security, and low interest rates that have decimated traditional sources of safe interest payments, the rules have been completely upended, and more often than not, not in your favor.

You are going to need help. This is complicated and technical, and fought with peril. Often you will have only one chance to get many of your choices right, and if you get them wrong, you, and perhaps your spouse, will have to live with them for a lifetime.

But, if you can get this one question right...how long you are going to live...or at least learn to navigate around it, you may be able to gain control of your future and have a safe and secure retirement in spite of Wall Street and the other forces lined up against you.

But as you cast about for advice, be careful.

> "There's a sucker born every minute."
> — Attributed to P.T. Barnum

About Fiduciaries (Maybe the #1 Secret Wall Street Hopes You Don't Find Out!)

I know top 10 lists and the like are supposed to count down to number one, however my thinking was that if you got nothing more out of this little book, this would be the most important information you could have. So I cheated, and made this the first thing you see, justifying it as part of the introduction.

But wait...I don't have to justify anything! It's my book. So, what are you waiting for...get started!

As an Investment Advisor Representative (IAR) with a series 65 securities license, we hold a fiduciary duty to you. This means that we are legally bound to put your interests above those of anyone else, including ourselves.

Now you might reasonably think that anyone offering financial advice to clients is required to be a fiduciary. Sadly, if you thought that, you'd be wrong. Some estimates claim that only 15% of advisors have a fiduciary responsibility. The Paladin Registry puts the number even lower, estimating that just one in 12 (8.3%) advisors have fiduciary responsibility.

For the most part, stockbrokers (also called "Registered Representatives," "Account Executives," "Financial Advisors" or "Wealth Managers") are not fiduciaries, even though they are allowed to portray themselves as full-service investment advisors. If your stockbroker/registered representative/account executive/financial advisor/wealth manager holds a series 7 securities license, then it's probable that they aren't a fiduciary.

Being a fiduciary is a legal distinction. A Registered Investment Advisor (RIA) or Investment Advisor Representative (IAR) who holds a series 65 securities license subject to the Investment Advisers Act of 1940, is a fiduciary. The legal investment advising standards that govern a non-fiduciary stockbroker and a fiduciary Registered Investment Advisor are very different.

A Registered Investment Advisor is required by law to follow the "trust" standard – the highest known in law – which requires it to place the interests of its clients ahead of its own and fulfill critical fiduciary duties of trust and confidence. Under the fiduciary trust standard, a Registered Investment Advisor must provide its "best advice" to a client. A non-fiduciary stockbroker follows only the "suitability" standard, which doesn't require a stockbroker to place the interests of its clients ahead of its own. Under the non-fiduciary suitability standard, a stockbroker need provide only "suitable advice" to its clients – even if the stockbroker knows that the advice is not the best advice for its client.

Even if a non-fiduciary stockbroker wanted to follow the trust standard of law and become a fiduciary to its clients, it cannot do so because of the contract it has with its broker-dealer. Such contracts require the stockbroker to place the interests of the broker-dealer before the interests of the stockbroker's clients. A stockbroker, then, owes fiduciary duties only to its broker-dealer – not to its investment clients. A Registered Investment Advisor owes fiduciary duties only to its investment clients because it doesn't have a broker-dealer.

The critical difference between a stockbroker and a Registered Investment Advisor is that the RIA is subject to the high fiduciary legal standard when providing investment advising services while the stockbroker is not. This difference could have a major impact on your investment portfolio and hence your retirement lifestyle.

Full disclosure (a component of the trust standard!) requires that I disclose that I am biased in this area. One of the reasons I never became a Series 6 or Series 7 representative is because I don't want an outside party telling me what I should be doing with my clients. In other words, if I truly believe it's in your best interest to go one way, and my broker/dealer was insisting, for "compliance purposes," that I provide you another solution and downplay or dismiss what I believe is the best answer for you, I want to have the freedom to do what is in your best interest without fear of losing my livelihood.

Series 6 and Series 7 representatives are often barred from doing that by their broker-dealers. Imagine a business model that requires you to do something that is not in your best interest?

Chances are you are currently involved in just such an arrangement. As I mentioned before, only 8% to 12% of advisors have a fiduciary responsibility to the client. That means that somewhere around 90% do not. What do you think the odds are you are working with a fiduciary? Right…around 10%!

How does this manifest itself in people's lives?

I recently ran across an article from the AP in our local paper. The headline read, "Investors lose billions in savings betting on energy partnerships." The article went on to report the story of a school teacher in Texas who had been widowed and was concerned about having enough money to raise her two young girls and have enough for retirement.

So, a financial services representative, portraying himself as a financial planner, recommended she put her money in energy partnerships that would allow her to ride the "shale oil boom," promising her high returns and a steady stream of payments to help cover her bills. The article reports that she liked him because of his confidence in the product, and she trusted him. Needless to say, within a very short time (two years), the client had lost half of her life savings.

The question becomes, of course, was he trustworthy? As a registered rep with a major financial services firm—one you would recognize—he had the cache of respectability and trust, without the responsibility. He was able to hitch himself to the wagon of respectability, trustworthiness and goodwill of the company's millions and millions of dollars in annual advertising, without having to deal with the legal responsibility of a fiduciary.

How do I know this? No fiduciary anywhere would put a person's livelihood in energy partnerships. Does that mean a fiduciary would never present them? Of course not. One might, after making sure that the client had allocated all of the secure income and growth needed, present energy partnerships as a place to put a portion of the money designated to high-risk growth. In this case a very small portion. Why? Because energy partnerships are extremely risky. Risky means likely to fail. In other words, this representative of a very well-known financial services giant recommended a widowed school teacher with two young children put her life savings in an arrangement which was more than likely to fail.

Does this sound like a person who was looking out for the needs of his client? Or does this sound like a person who was more interested in hawking the products being promoted by his company and the lucrative commissions that brought to him? Who in this arrangement was looking out for the client? No one is who.

Had this family been my client a couple of things would have happened. First, I would have insisted, as a condition of working with me, that the husband, while still alive, have enough life insurance to take care of his family if something should happen to him. That does not mean he had to buy life insurance from me...it just means he had to have enough life insurance to take care of his family if he wanted my advice and guidance. This is standard practice for us. When a client works with me, they have to have the basics...wills, trusts, survivorship planning, etc., covered. In fact, we offer very reasonably priced access to legal services right in our office for this very reason.

The next thing that would have happened would have been how the money would have been allocated after he died. We would never have recommended she put her life savings in energy partnerships. I would have insisted she put her money in a savings arrangement that would have kept her money safe, provided a reasonable rate of return, and been available to her and her family when needed. I wish for her sake her advisor had done just that. She and her young daughters would have been much better off.

Lessons from the street

Do you collect people? More to the point, do you collect service professionals? Here's what I mean.

Last week a couple, call them Ben and Judy, who had been to one of our Social Security workshops held at schools around New England, came in to see me afterward. Now this isn't unusual; most of the people who attend come in to talk about their retirement income plans. Some even come in just to talk about Social Security, and that's okay. But this couple came in to talk to me as "the Social Security guy."

As I dug a little deeper I learned why they thought of me this way. It turned out they already have a "financial planner" (the guy who buys and sells their stocks), an insurance guy, an accountant, an attorney, someone they refer to when they need advice on their employer-sponsored retirement plan (their "retirement guy"), etc. So now I was their "Social Security guy." So as not to disappoint them I ran their Social Security illustration and showed them the most efficient way to elect, and as I did so I could see the consternation written on their faces. By far the most efficient way for this couple to take their benefits was to wait until later to elect—to the tune of over $150,000! The problem was, the "plan" they were putting together with the help of three or four of these other people called for them to take it immediately. Essentially they had come to me to bless that plan.

"We want to have our money sooner rather than later," Judy said.

"Yeah, while we can enjoy it," echoed Ben. "We're planning to retire at 62, enjoy life while we can, and then by the time we're old and feeble we won't need that much money anyway. Our financial planner agrees with us," he continued. "Our plan is to move our entire 401k into his management company as soon as we do retire. He's the one who told us to take Social Security as soon as possible."

"So does our accountant," said Judy. "She told us to hold off on using our 401(k)s and then take as little as possible so we can save on taxes. That way we can leave more to our kids. But to do that we need to take Social Security as soon as we can get it."

"Our lawyer's on board, too," Judy said, picking up momentum. "He has set us up with a trust and a 'pour-over' will. The trust is the beneficiary of our 401(k)s and also all of our other assets when we die. He says that's the most efficient way to set things up, and he's agreed to be trustee so we don't have to worry about that."

As if playing the trump card, Ben finished with, "Even our insurance guy is in agreement. He's recommended we purchase a variable annuity with the money my parents left me, and he says it fits right in with our plan."

Ben and Judy fell quiet and stared at me as if to say, "What do you think of *that*, Mr. Social Security guy?"

"What I think is," I explained, "is that you have way too many cooks in the kitchen. Rather than having a different advisor for every different piece of your plan, you should have one advisor acting as sort of a head coach, helping coordinate your entire plan. Then you would not be running into some of the mistakes you are making."

"What mistakes?" they chimed in unison. "We have several different people who are all agreeing with each other."

"Well first," I said, "is your Social Security election. Two or three of your 'advisors' have told you the best thing for you was to take it as early as possible. We've already demonstrated that has the potential of costing you up to $150,000 or more in lifetime benefits. How can that be a good thing? It looks to me like your current advisors either don't know any better or believe waiting would not be in their best interest.

"Next you have a 'financial planner' who sees the opportunity to take all of your 401(k) money under management. Of course he's going to endorse the plan. It works in his best interest. In addition, you've got a lawyer who has set you up so that as soon as both of you are gone he can probate your entire estate…even the portion that should be in the trust will be probated. In addition, he has recommended he be the trustee, meaning he gets to control all your assets after you've gone, including your tax-qualified retirement plans which should pass by beneficiary designation directly to your beneficiaries.

"What would *you* suggest?" they asked. So I told them.

"First, I would fire your lawyer and find one who has your best interests at heart. Second, I would use the Social Security analysis we ran as a baseline income plan. We already know that if one of you lives past life expectancy—of which there is greater than 80% chance—this will provide you the most money from a guaranteed asset. Further, that money lasts for as long as either of you is alive, so it makes sense to maximize it.

"Then, I would look at ways to maximize your qualified money by reducing or eliminating taxes from it. We have a couple options: the "Free Money™ Roth Transfer" in which we can recapture most, if not all, of the taxes you pay to convert, or the "IRA 590™" which allows you to take two to three times as much as your RMD allows without drawing down any of your IRA account, and then leave the full amount to your beneficiaries tax-free. Either of the strategies would allow you to enjoy much more of your tax qualified retirement accounts, dramatically reduce the taxes to your kids, and maybe even reduce taxes on your Social Security benefits.

"I would steer clear of a variable annuity, but I would investigate all of the guaranteed income strategies available to ensure that you never run out of money, no matter how long either of you live. You want to get out of a situation where you are relying on market-risk products for income. Any money left you could feel free to invest any way you like, *after* you have ensured you have enough money to live your life out in comfort and security."

"Finally, I would make sure whoever is advising you is acting in a fiduciary role, where your interests are put first. Only by having someone who both understands and has visibility into your entire financial picture, and is required by law to put your interests over theirs, can you get solid, knowledgeable advice that's designed to work in your best interest."

Not bad for a "Social Security guy"!

And now, to all those *other* secrets Wall Street doesn't want you to know…

> "It could probably be shown by facts and figures that there is no distinctly native American criminal class except Congress."
> — Mark Twain

Big Secret #10: 401(k)s were not done for you, they were done to you.

"I would blow up the system and restart with something totally different.... Now this monster is out of control."

—Ted Benna, the "father" of the 401(k)[3]

This was one of the biggest disruptions to our retirement planning system to ever come about, and like so many of the things that Congress does to mess up our lives was completely unintended and not thought out. Prior to the 1980s retirement was more of a collective endeavor rather than an individual one.

---

[3] Smith, Hedrick (2012-09-11). Who Stole the American Dream? (Kindle Locations 2731-2732). Random House Publishing Group. Kindle Edition.

First of all, many people actually had pensions. Pensions are based on a promise: you devote a lifetime of service to one or two employers, and in turn, those employers would take care of you after your service is complete. This was what is known as a social covenant, or promise, or pledge. It was a contract between the worker and the employer, and it goes back to Roman times when Roman soldiers would end their service and retire to their farms and family businesses, but with a pension, or "annua," that would be paid for life. Later, in 225 A.D., Ulpianus, a Roman judge, formulated the first know mortality table for lifetime payouts from a lump sum payment.[4]

The first private pension plan in the United States was established in 1875 by the American Express Company. Prior to that they did not exist as most U.S. businesses were small, family-run enterprises. By 1940, 4.1 million private-sector workers were covered by pension plans, and by 1950, 9.8 million, or 25% of all private-sector workers were covered.[5] Pensions continued to grow in popularity until in 1980 over 60% of employed Americans participated in over 165,000 pensions.[6]

---

[4] Hegna, Tom. "Annuity Timeline - They Are Older than You Think." In *Pay Checks and Play Checks: Retirement Solutions for Life*. Boston, MA.: Acanthus Publishing, 2011.

[5] "History of Pension Plans." Fact March 1998 | EBRI. Accessed 2015. http://www.ebri.org/publications/facts/index.cfm?fa=0398afact.

[6] Richard Rubin and Margaret Collins, "You Can Thank or Blame Richard Stanger for Writing 401(k)", Bloomberg Business Online, Feb 3, 2014

One of the things about pensions that made them such a powerful safety net for people was the fact that lifespan was a non-issue for them. Like Social Security, pensions pay people for their whole lifespan. As long as you live, you will be paid your benefit. This is huge, and it's the only way to deal with uncertain lifespans and the danger of living too long. They completely eliminate the "When are you going to die" issue. We will deal with this on a more detailed level throughout this book.

Moreover, our parents grew up as Depression babies. They had a clear recollection, either of their own, or first-hand accounts, of the toll the Great Depression took on their parents and families. Our parents grew up as workers and savers. Home ownership was a dream, not an expectation. The idea of devoting one's life to a single employer was not foreign to them. In fact, it embodied the American Dream: work hard all your life, save, spend wisely, pass on a better America to your kids, and in turn, the system will provide the basic requirements of a short, but sweet retirement. This became especially true after the passage of the Social Security Act of 1934. That wasn't the only thing that emerged from the Great Depression, however.

Just prior to that, in 1932 and 1933, Congress passed the Banking Acts of 1932 and 1933, also known collectively as Glass-Steagall, named for its two sponsors, Senator Carter Glass (D) of Virginia, and Representative Henry B. Steagall (D) of Alabama. The primary thrust of this legislation was to create a firewall between investment banking and commercial banking, which prior to that had not existed. Not having that protection meant that commercial banks—those banks where ordinary people deposit their savings, were authorized to, and did profusely, gamble those savings in highly speculative and risky investments. This led to the Crash of 1929, when the additional lack of protections for depositors—such as lack of deposit insurance, and the lack of foreclosure protections, in turn led to the Great Depression.

Altogether the Banking Acts of 1932 and 1933, along with the Social Security Act of 1934, and the establishment of the GI Bill and other reforms before and after the war, led to a time of unprecedented financial growth and prosperity. The American Dream had become manifestly real.

Then things started to change. Banks began to lobby heavily to engage in more securities transactions, ultimately leading to the repeal of Glass-Steagall in 1999 under the Gramm–Leach–Bliley Act. In addition, in 1978, another seminal act was passed by Congress: the Revenue Act of 1978.

Deferred compensation arrangements ("cash or deferred arrangements," known as CODAs), which allowed some compensation (and resulting tax liability) to be deferred, had been in existence for decades and are commonly viewed as the predecessors to the 401(k) plan. Due to concerns about revenue collection, there was much effort by the IRS to restrict the tax deferral of such plans. In 1974,

Congress barred the IRS from restricting the tax-deferred status of these plans with the Employee Retirement Income Security Act of 1974 (ERISA), and mandated that all employees should be provided the same options—not just highly-compensated executives.

Then, in 1978, the earth moved. No one felt it. In fact, no one but a very few people in Congress and some highly-paid executives in upstate NY even knew about it. But move it did. The story goes like this. Highly paid executives at Xerox and Kodak in Rochester, NY were looking for a way to shelter bonus money from taxes.

> In the pivotal Congress of 1978, as we have seen, the 401(k) was inserted into the tax code like many arcane technical provisions, as a favor to Kodak, Xerox, and a few New York banks by Representative Barber Conable, a Republican from upstate New York. His district housed the Kodak and Xerox headquarters, and the two companies lobbied Conable hard to protect a pet tax break. Their CEOs were fighting to stop the Treasury Department from killing a previously established tax shelter for executives and rank-and-file employees who choose (sic) to save profit-sharing bonuses for retirement. To stop that tax bite, Kodak's lawyer, Carroll Savage, wrote out verbatim the language for 401(k) and passed it to Conable.

> As the ranking Republican on the tax-writing House Ways and Means Committee, Conable was perfectly positioned to tuck the 401(k) provision into a major tax bill as a tiny subparagraph. It was a classic Washington move. Almost no one else in Congress or the Carter White House even noticed.[7]

In fact, it received no discussion or debate at all. None. Zero. Nada. I have often said the 401(k) was not something that was done for us. It was done *to* us. Xerox, Kodak and the rest of corporate America were not the only culprits. Wall Street and the mutual fund industry were also in the thick of things. The industry immediately saw the opportunity and aggressively marketed the plans as a money saving strategy for business, and rapidly pulled corporate America away from pensions and into 401(k)s.

This was a monumental transformation for the American middle class.

> When the 401(k)'s (sic) came in, there was a sea change, a huge shift in who was paying for retirement. In the old system, employers put up most of the money— 89 percent. The employees contributed 11 percent. Those figures are from the Department of Labor. Fast-forward to the 401(k) system and today,

---

[7] Smith, Hedrick (2012-09-11). Who Stole the American Dream? (Kindle Locations 2741-2765). Random House Publishing Group. Kindle Edition.

employees are paying more than half— 51 percent—
and the companies, 49 percent. So there was a huge
shift in costs from employers to employees—
hundreds of billions of dollars.[8]

These plans took off like a rocket. As corporate America and Wall Street began sniffing the dollars to be had, they became relentless in pushing these plans onto unsuspecting workers. The lure of "being your own money manager" was too great a temptation to resist, and millions of Americans bought in. Defined contribution plans like the 401(k), 403(b), IRA, etc. grew rapidly, from 7 million people with $92 billion in assets in 1984 to 44 million people with nearly $3 trillion in 2004.

All this new money in the markets bid up prices as well, while the actual number of securities in the American exchanges has shrunk from a high of 8,823 companies in 1997 to 5,091 in 2007[9], and under 5,000 in 2013. The number of mutual funds exploded as well, from 564 available in 1980 at the birth of the 401(k), to 8,155 funds in 2000. The number of funds has gone down some while the total number of equities shrinks, with around 7.900 still in existence in 2014. However the true story is told by the number of share classes, which has increased steadily over the years from 1,243 in 1984 to over 24,000 in 2014. Even more telling, the amount of money

---

[8] Ibid
[9] Grant Thorton

flowing into these funds has exploded from $134 billion in 1980 to $6.96 trillion in 2000 and $7.923 trillion in 2014.

So what does this all mean? With the migration of the Baby Boomer retirement funds away from safely managed pensions and into the markets, the growing number of investors and investor dollars has dramatically bid up the price of what otherwise might be considered a shrinking market. In other words, stocks, which used to be valued based on the health and value of the companies that issued them, have become valued based on what they will bring in the market. How else could a company like Apple, which has virtually no capital infrastructure other than its buildings, become the highest-valued company in the world, beating out such giants as GM, Ford, GE, etc.?

In effect, it was a party. No one looked twice at the fact that defined-benefit plans were disappearing at an alarming rate, nor was anyone concerned that America's retirement was moving wholesale into the casino. The casino was roaring forward. Payouts were massive. It ushered in a new age when corporate profits didn't matter anymore. All you needed was a "dot-com" in the name and you were going to be rich. Everyone, it seemed, was on board with the wholesale dismantling and raiding of the American retirement system. In fact, it became such a popular idea that after the 2004 presidential election, the Bush administration made the privatization of Social Security its number-one economic agenda item. Thankfully, there were cooler heads in the mix, and in the end, they prevailed.

What happens to the value of these companies as money starts to exit the market? We've all been riding this wave of Boomer retirement-fueled new capital into the market. But what happens as we Boomers begin to retire and sell off our holdings? Does their value start to go down?

Bob, Alice, Ted and Carol

Meet Bob. Bob is married to Alice. Bob and Alice have been married for 40 years. They have three well-adjusted kids, all of whom they put through college. They have six grandchildren, each of whom have a college fund that was started by Bob and Alice. Bob is 66 and Alice is 64. After a productive and fruitful working life they are ready to retire. They have no idea what that means, but they are feeling pretty good.

Together, they have saved about $1.2 million. In addition, Bob's Social Security benefit will be around $30,000 a year, and Alice's will be around $20,000. They are currently spending around $120,000 a year to live and have been under the impression they would be able to maintain very close to that during their retirement.

Bob and Alice go to a financial planner to confirm their plan and find out the best way to achieve the results they are seeking. His name is Dick.

Dick recommends that they start taking Social Security as soon as possible. He reasons that they have to live well into their 70s to get to the break-even point, and by taking more money up front they will be able to grow their nest egg more. Dick believes he can conservatively get them between 8% and 10% rates of return, and he believes they will be able to safely pull around six percent a year from their savings with a three percent inflation adjustment each year. After all, the market has been growing dramatically over the past couple of decades and it looks like there is no end in sight.

So Bob and Alice are on their way. The next year they receive about $50,000 a year from Social Security and another $70,000 a year from their investments, and retirement is grand. Bob has an old $500,000 life policy with about $40,000 in cash value that he is tired of paying premiums on. So he decides to cash it in and take the whole family on a European trip. That's one none of them will ever forget! And why not? He is, as he likes to remind Alice quite frequently, a millionaire. The date is September 11, 1999, and the stock market is booming with no end in sight.

By the end of 1999, everything is still going strong, so Bob and Alice purchase that condo in Florida that they've always wanted. Their wealth continues to grow and is now at around $1.44 million in spite of the extra $30,000 they had to take out for the down payment on the condo. With all that extra money they keep earning in the market, it seems that they will have enough for anything they want. Retirement truly is grand!

It's two years later and everything has changed. No one could have anticipated this! The world came to a standstill as the horror of September 11, 2001 unfolded. People were certain the United States was under attack. Planes were grounded. Troops were called up. The president remained in Air Force One on a war footing, and the vice president was in the White House bunker contemplating shooting airliners out of the sky.

These few years are disastrous for Bob and Alice. Their portfolio has dropped from a high of $1.44 million to about $722,000. Fifty percent gone in just two years! That Florida condo is a real drain, and they are finding it very difficult to cut back, especially since their oldest son lost his job and the family is now living in their basement. It was either that or end up on the streets. No one is real happy about it, but you do what you have to do.

One good thing has happened however. He followed Dick's advice, left his money in the market when he really wanted to pull it all out. The market has been rebounding, but Bob is worried the $85,000 it's costing to live every year is going to weaken his ability to rebound with it. But, it's holding steady, and as long as the market continues to hold, they should have enough to get by.

A year later it's 2008 and the sky has fallen. Not only is what's left of his portfolio way down, to under $400,000 and sinking, he is underwater in both his houses. They've had to let the Florida condo go because they simply can't afford the payments any longer. They don't dare sell their residence as that has lost a huge amount of value as well. Anyway, if they did, where would they live?

…

Meet Ted. Ted is married to Carol. Ted and Carol have been married for 40 years. They have two great kids, and four grands. Together, they have saved about $1.4 million. In addition, Ted's Social Security benefit will be around $30,000 a year, and Carol's will be around $20,000. They are currently spending around $120,000 a year to live and have been under the impression they will be able to maintain very close to that during their retirement. After all, they are millionaires aren't they? The date is September 11, 2015…

"People say they love truth, but in reality they want to believe that which they love is true." — Robert Ringer

Big Secret #9: Tax deferral is often a tax trap

Although everyone agrees that eliminating taxes is a great way to save money, no one really knows how to do it. The conventional wisdom of the day holds that tax-deferred retirement accounts like 401(k)s, IRAs, 403(b)s, etc. are great ways to save taxes. Heck, most CPAs and financial planners I know believe this. What people often fail to consider, however, is when you defer taxes, you are also deferring the tax rate. In addition, you are growing the balance upon which you will be paying taxes. The trap, of course, is you could be setting yourself up for having to pay a higher tax on more money, not to mention what it can do to things like taxes on your Social Security benefits.

As an example, assume you are just starting out in life, and you are able to max out your IRA contributions at $5,000 a year, and that number will hold steady throughout your career. Assuming an 8% rate of growth, you will have saved $616,729 by the time you're ready to retire at age 65, and at a 15% tax rate, you will have accrued $92,509 of taxes on that money which you will now have to pay during retirement, meaning you will have a net total value of $524,220 in your traditional IRA account.

Now compare that to a Roth IRA, where instead of deferring the taxes and the tax rate, you went ahead and paid the taxes each year at the 15% tax rate. It should come as no surprise that at the end of the term, you will have exactly the same amount in your account net of taxes, $524,220. The reason for this is because if taxes remain constant, there is no difference between paying the taxes before your money grows versus after your money grows as long as the growth rate remains the same for both cases.

Alternatively, let's assume that the tax rate did not remain steady, rather it grew by .2% per year. At the end of that 35-year period, the tax rate will have increased from 15% to 26.64%. Consider that if you had waited until the very end to pay taxes, you would have had to pay 26.64% on all of the money accrued during that 35 year period of time, which would have left a net result of $452,447 after taxes.

However, had you had a Roth IRA or other tax-free accumulation account during that period of time you would have been paying the taxes at each year's lesser rate. For example, year one, you would have only paid 15%. Year two, you would have paid 15.3%, and so forth. Only at the very end of your working life would you have approached the 26.64% rate to which if finally grew. Doing it this way your money would have grown to $559,675, or $107,228 more than the conventional IRA. That's almost 24% more money over the same period of time.

That's not the end of the story, however. For example, in the case of the tax-deferred approach, you will be forced to pay taxes on income derived from your retirement savings throughout your retirement. This could mean you will have to pay taxes on benefits such as Social Security, which you may have otherwise been able to avoid.

As an example, assume you and your spouse have accrued enough Social Security credits to begin retirement with a $40,000 annual benefit. Since you have deferred all of the taxes as well as the tax rate on your retirement plan income, your provisional income level is such that you have to pay taxes on 50% of your Social Security benefit at 26.64%, making taxes on your Social Security benefits $5,328 during the first year alone. Assuming no tax rate increase for the entire term of your retirement, but with a 2.8% annual cost-of-living increase for Social Security, total taxes paid on your Social Security benefits after 25 years will be $189,217.

(It should be noted that if the provisional income is high enough – $34k annually for a single person, and $44k annually for a married couple – 85% of Social Security benefits will be taxed rather than just 50%. Also, while you are considering this, consider this as well. Social

Security benefits are the only retirement benefits that are actually taxed twice. That's right, while Congress has been busy steeling our Social Security trust fund over the years, it also set it up so that not only do you pay the premium (your Social Security payroll tax) with after-tax dollars, in 1983 it changed the law that had been in existence since Social Security was originally passed stating Social Security would never be subject to federal income tax.)

Add that $189,217 of unnecessary Social Security taxes to the additional $107,228 of additional taxes you paid on your retirement savings due to the tax rate increases over time, and that's $296,445 of additional taxes you will have to pay over your retirement lifetime simply because you followed the conventional wisdom. Put another way, over a 25-year retirement, you lost just under $12,000 a year in tax-free income because you followed the herd. Further, due to the way they are calculated, the additional taxes on your Social Security may well have had to be paid whether the tax rates went up or not, just due to delaying them until your retirement years.

Does this sound like a reasonable deal to you? Would this necessarily be the case in your situation? Will taxes go up over time or down? I honestly don't know. However, I do know that it's not as simple as people would like you to think it is. Yes, deferring taxes to a future point in time sounds like a good idea when you are young and making money. However, it may pay to sit back and look at the whole picture before making the decision about something you may have to live with for the rest of your life.

One thing I do know. This arrangement has been just fine for Wall Street and the people who have held our money hostage for the past 35 years.

"Men occasionally stumble over the truth, but most of them pick themselves up and hurry off as if nothing ever happened."
— Winston S. Churchill

Big Secret #8: Gravity cannot be ignored.

Gravity. Often it can be used for our benefit. Sometimes it can be defended against, or even overcome temporarily. But it can never be ignored.

For centuries man longed to fly like the birds. Thousands of contraptions were invented over time, but with the exception ballooning, nothing broke through until December 17, 1903 in Kitty Hawk, NC. Since that time flight has literally and figuratively soared beyond the wildest dreams of man. However, one thing has never changed. No matter how far and fast we go, unless we break the bounds of Earth, gravity will always win out. Even then, it cannot be ignored. In fact, it's gravity that holds the very universe together and makes its very existence possible. The jet plane that is soaring through the air is just a tankful of jet fuel away from crashing into this unforgiving reality.

If we look closely we can determine the gravitational pull in other areas, too. In the market, economic fundamentals create a gravity as powerful and certain as the attraction between the planets. By understanding these gravitational forces at play, one can make determinations about what the market is apt to do over time.

If you consider the current market within this historical context, it's easy to determine that the gravitational pull is down. Take a look at two separate, though similar, measurements: the price to earnings ratio (PE), and the market cap to gross domestic product (GDP) ratio. Both of these forces act on the market with the certainty of the gravitational pull between the planets and stars.

The PE ratio is a measurement of the earnings of a company with respect to its market value. The PE can also be applied to groups of stock, indexes, and the market as a whole. The market cap to GDP ratio is the measurement of the total output of an economic sector or nation with respect to its total market value. Both of these metrics are understandable at a fundamental level. By all rights, as a company makes more in profits, its market value should rise, and vice versa. The same applies to an economy's total output. The more an economy produces, the more it should be worth.

Sometimes markets will behave in an anticipatory way and try to predict an outcome. Traders will identify a market sector or economy they believe will take off and invest heavily in anticipation of huge profits. Due to the emotional and often irrational nature of investor behavior, primarily driven by two primal forces – fear and greed – these instances can take on lives of their own. However, as in the tech bubble of the 1990s, these are rarely real, and gravity will always win out. Nobel Laureate Robert Shiller has made this point repeatedly in his multiple editions of the classic on behavioral economics, "Irrational Exuberance," predicting with chilling accuracy the crashes of 2001 and 2008.

If you look at the center of gravity in today's market you will observe by all metrics it is significantly over-valued. In fact, in a historical context, it is positioned for a fall just as surely as that jet plane when it is out of fuel. According to both metrics cited above, today's market is significantly overvalued. If you look back, you will see that the last three times the market cap to GDP ratio was this overvalued were in 1972, 2000 and 2007, immediately before three of the worst market crashes in history.

In Figure1, below, the market cycles are depicted by the bar chart, and the PE ratios are illustrated by the blue line at the bottom. There are three numbers on the left: 0, 15, and 25. Along the bottom are the years 1900 to present. Looking at the PE ratio, we notice some disturbing indicators. Going back to the turn of the 20th Century, it is possible to track secular bull and bear markets to levels of the PE ratio.

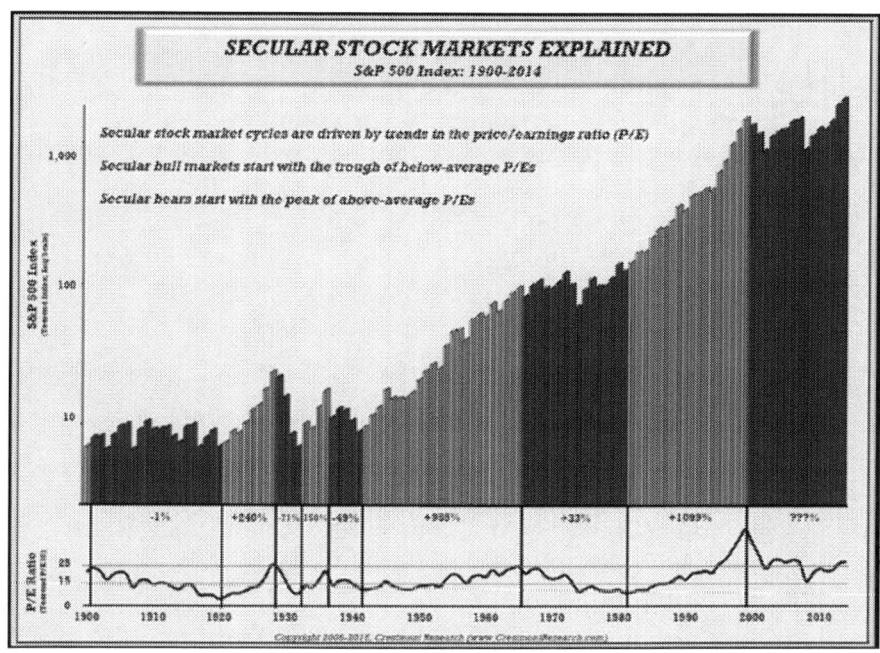

Figure 1: Secular Stock Market explained from Crestmont Research

Never, in the history of the modern stock market has a true bull market recovery occurred while PE ratios were over 15. And every time the overall market cap reached 25 or more, there was a significant crash. What's the current PE ratio? Twenty four point five (24.5). What should that tell you?[10]

There's more. Like an after-burner on a rocket, a recent "non-announcement" of interest rate hike caused the Dow to soar by over 300 points in one day. Think about that. The Fed did nothing to indicate it would or would not raise rates over the next quarter, year,

---

[10] Easterling, Ed. "Are We There Yet? Secular Stock Market Cycle Status." Crestmont Research (2015). Print.

or decade. It simply did not raise rates in this one meeting, and made no announcement either way.

The "Irrational Exuberance" of the investing public kicked in and the market soared, in spite of the fact that stocks are significantly overvalued, in spite of the fact that interest rates are still at record lows and will have to…must…with 100% certainty…come back up at some time in the probably not too distant future, in spite of the fact that we are sitting on the third significant economic bubble in the past 15 years, and in spite of the fact that we've all been through this before and know, without a doubt, what is coming. In spite of all these things, all of the passengers on the plan have crowded into first class and everyone is having a party instead of looking for a safe place to land.

Further, the market is ever more precarious every single day. Refer back to those low interest rates previously discussed, and remember how low they are, and have been, since the Crash of 2008. Here's what Warren Buffett has to say about interest rates and the market.

> Interest rates "act on financial valuations the way gravity acts on matter: The higher the rate, the greater the downward pull. That's because the rates of return that investors need from any kind of investment are directly tied to the risk-free rate that they can earn from government securities. So if the government rate rises, the prices of all other investments must

adjust downward, to a level that brings their expected rates of return into line. Conversely, if government interest rates fall, the move pushes the prices of all other investments upward."[11]

Currently the Federal Reserve has kept interest rates at record lows for over five years. What happens when it stops, and interest rates rise? It will bring the market crashing down.

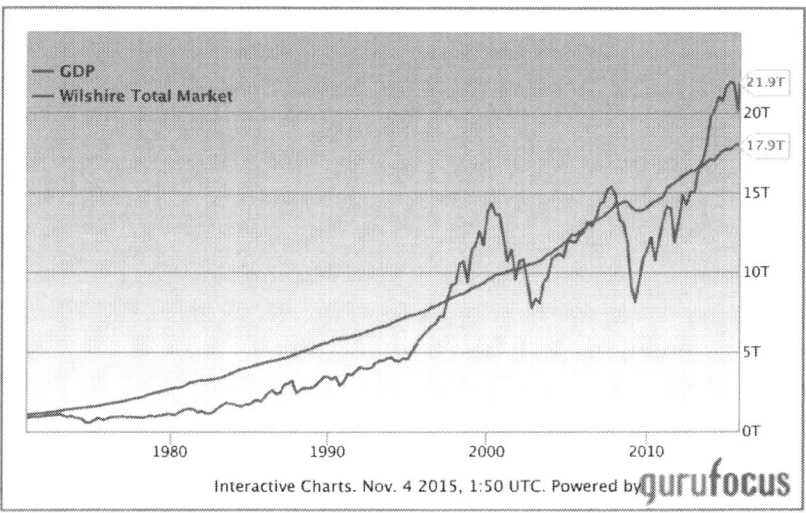

Figure 2: GDP to Wilshire Total Market Cap Ratio

Interest rates would probably not have as much impact if the market were stable. Is it though? We've already seen how the market has been bid up over the past couple of decades by Boomer retirement accounts. But how over-valued is it really?

---

[11] http://www.gurufocus.com/stock-market-valuations.php

Figure 2 shows the Market Cap to GDP Ratio. As I write this, it stands at 120.8%. Take a look at the last two times this ratio was so high, in 2000 and 2008. What happened then? As such, it is significantly overvalued, according to the following table[12]:

Ratio = Total Market Cap / GDP	Valuation
Ratio < 50%	Significantly Undervalued
50% < Ratio < 75%	Modestly Undervalued
75% < Ratio < 90%	Fair Valued
90% < Ratio < 115%	Modestly Overvalued
Ratio > 115%	Significantly Overvalued
Where are we today (11/03/2015)?	Ratio = 122.2%, **Significantly Overvalued**

Figure 3: GDP to Market Cap Legend

How long can this be sustained? Is the bond bubble we are now in greater than previous bubbles? How about the derivatives market. Surely that's changed, right? It's estimated that the world's four largest banks hold between them $216.5 trillion in derivatives. Since we are on a roll with Buffett, he has said derivatives are "financial weapons of mass destruction," carrying "potentially lethal" dangers within them.

The signs, if you look for them are there. As surely as the fuel gauge on the jet about to fall from the sky. The passengers are oblivious because they don't have access to the gauges, and the pilots are distracted. In the end, however, gravity will win out. It has too. But, in the meantime...

---

[12] Ibid

"Facts do not cease to exist because they are ignored."
— Aldous Huxley

Big Secret #7: Wall Street counts on your complacency.

It's true. Wall Street and its agents know that most people are motivated by emotions, not rational thought. After all, it people were rational, they would be getting out of the market now, rather than pouring money in. Why do I say that? Take a look at this chart of the S&P 500 from January 1990 to October 2015:

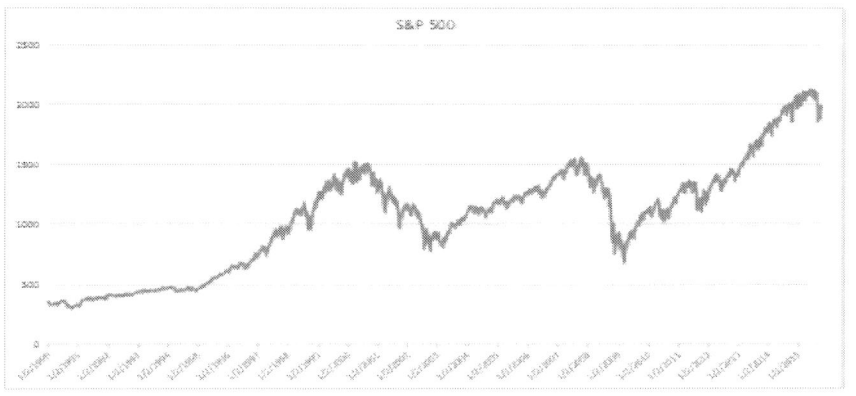

Figure 4: S&P 500: January 1990 to October 2015

Now step back. Exhale. Take the emotion out of it. What is this chart screaming at you in 10 feet high capital letters? Buy or sell?

There is even and index that measures investor complacency. It's called the Volatility Index, or VIX. Following is a chart from Yahoo Finance showing the VIX from January 2008 to present.

As you might imagine, volatility is a measure of investor behavior, or complacency. When markets are high investors become very complacent. They believe that life is good, it will always be good, and nothing can upset the apple cart. So, when investors are complacent, the VIX is very low. Take a look at the VIX in May 2008 (A). Stocks were at an all-time high. Where was the VIX? Where is it now? (B) This means we are very, very complacent.

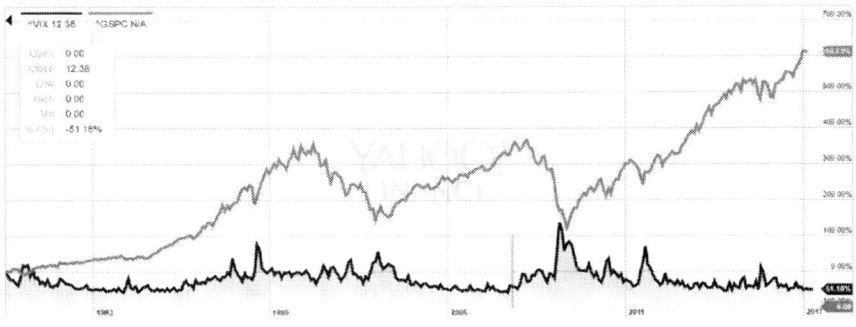

Figure 5: Volatility Index (VIX)

What's all this mean? It means the financial services and investing industry incredibly complex, opaque, and in many instances corrupt. It is virtually unpoliced and unregulated, or able to be regulated. More often than not, its crimes and shenanigans surface after the incredible damage is done, as in 2008 when trillions of dollars vanished and millions of lives were damaged. No one went to jail, and the following year Wall Street mavens enjoyed one of the biggest annual bonuses in history, compliments of the U.S. government. And your money is still in the hands of the very people who brought us the financial disasters of the last two decades, with the next one seemingly right around the corner, all while we fiddle while Rome burns. Talk about complacency!

"It's very difficult to make predictions, especially about the future."
— Yogi Berra

Big Secret #6: Wall Street hasn't a clue what to do.

Back in the mid 90's a planner from San Diego by the name of William Bengen determined that a retiree could prudently begin retirement by withdrawing 4% from savings, and then add a 3% inflation adjustment each year, and expect to have enough money for 30 years of retirement, utilizing a 50/50 mix of stocks and bonds. He derived these numbers by looking at 75 years of prior data and modeling retirements of up to 50 years, commencing in every one of those 75 years. For years which would put retirement out into the future, he assumed business as usual for the first decade of the 21st Century.

Later, software vendors started incorporating "Monte Carlo" algorithms into their software to wow advisors and fool clients, using the same, faulty data from the past, and surprise, they came up with similar results. Monte Carlo planning is a stochastic method of measuring statistical randomness in a population which was first employed by physicists at the Manhattan Project. By introducing random outside influences and measuring the response, the process can produce highly accurate statistical outcomes based on various inputs. Sometimes. For example, it worked extremely well for nuclear physics because nuclear particles are governed by the laws of physics, and strict laws of nature can be relied upon to provide consistent results.

Financial income planning, however, has no such constrains. Things that influence economics include things that are entirely random and unpredictable. How, for example, could any software algorithm predict a tech bubble and an attack on the Twin Towers would occur at the same time? Or that the legislation that very effectively insulated bank depositors from aggressive speculation of their deposits would be repealed after 60 years of working spectacularly well? How can inputting variables from the past in any way predict what might happen in the future. For example, how could anything that happened in the early years of the 20th Century have anything to do with what might happen in the beginning of the 21st?

It is so much different than nuclear physics it's laughable. Randomness is, in a funny way, predictable. With physics we can bombard with specific radiation, heat something up, cool it down, compress it, expand it, and a thousand other things that we know about and are predictable.

Consistent with the basic theme of this book, the other thing missed by people who employ Monte Carlo planning for retirement planning is the statistical element that actually can be measured and predicted with scientific precision, and that's mortality (that when are you going to die thing). As posited throughout this book, of the main things that creates the most problems for financial planners is lifespan. How long one has to plan for has a huge impact on how you plan. For example, if you had $500,000 in your retirement account and you knew you were only going to live for 18 years, vs. 30 years, would that change the way you approached the plan? Of course it would. And this is something that Monte Carlo planning completely ignores, however it is this very thing that has made trillions of dollars for the life insurance industry. More about that later.

Lest you believe I am just making up the ineffectiveness of the Monte Carlo approach, consider this. No government regulating body, including FINRA, the SEC, the CFPB, or any state finance department will evaluate, let alone certify, any of these software programs, as they are regarded as completely bogus. If you are using a planner who utilizes these tools, you might want to run for the hills. After asking him or her how the trenches or World War I relate to the dot-com bubble, of course.

Nevertheless, Wall Street (risky) advisors glommed onto these planning "tools" (Monte Carlo and the 4% Rule) because it's all they had. Really. No one knew. No one had a clue. 401(k)s, if you will remember, were only around a decade old when the 4% Rule was created. How on earth could anyone give it any credence, especially those people who were putting their entire retirement security on the line?

Now Monte Carlo simulation (I call it Las Vegas planning), has for several years maintained that you can take about 4% of your savings each year with a 3% annual inflation increase and have a 90% chance of not running out of money before you die.

And somehow that's been acceptable. Only 10% of the time will you run out of money! What does that mean, really? It means that 10% of the time you are 100% up a creek! 10% of the time you are eating cat food. 10% of the time you don't get medicine. 10% of the time you freeze in your home...for the rest of your life (you are out of money...get it?). It does not mean that you just cut back 10%, which is what they would like you to think.

But the people employing these programs are, after all, risk-based (risky?) planners, meaning they are used to taking risks (read: gambling) with your money, so in their minds 10% isn't so bad. And this model worked pretty well until the last decade, when reality (read: gravity) reared its ugly head.

Did Somebody Say Crash (twice!)?

Now that reality has happened and we've had two total financial meltdowns within a single decade, with another apparently right around the corner, all of that past data is being shown for what it is: nonsense. It turns out that when you have frequent and drastic market downturns income planning isn't so cut and dried. In fact, a prominent study by T. Rowe Price (that you will never hear of...except here!) has determined that after the first decade of this century, the best case scenario is a 43% chance of success (success as defined as not being totally broke) when taking 4% a year with a 3% COLA. And that's only if you are willing to reduce your payout by 25% for three years after each market bottom. If you continue the original plan without making adjustments, you are faced with a 94% failure rate (94% of the time you are totally hosed!).

See the results of the study below.[13]

---

[13] Dismal Decade Offers Cautionary Lessons for Retirees, Study authored by T. Rowe Price, 1/2011

Account Status	Portfolio Value	Monthly Withdrawal Amount	Odds of Success*	Odds of Success After Bear Market Ended March 2009
At retirement on Jan. 1, 2000	$500,000	$1,667	89%	
Results as of December 31, 2010, Assuming Four Different Strategies				
Option 1: Continue withdrawals as planned	$334,578	$2,307	29%	6%
Option 2: Best Outcome Reduced withdrawals by 25% for three years after each bear market bottom	386,113	1,493	84	43
Option 3 Take no annual inflation adjustments for three years after each bear market bottom	352,367	1,990	69	26
Option 4: Worst Outcome Switched to 100% bond portfolio after first bear market bottom on October 1, 2002	270,669	2,307	0	0

Source: T. Rowe Price Associates

*Represents the percentage of total simulations in which the investor does not run out of money during a 30-year retirement period. The odds of success on January 1, 2000, reflect the initial investment and withdrawal assumptions. The odds of success at the various stages of the options reflect historical return data and any changes in the investment or withdrawal assumptions and projections thereafter. For historical returns, the S&P 500 Index is used for stocks and the Barclays Capital U.S. Aggregate Index is used for bonds. For simulations, stocks are expected to return 10% overall with a standard deviation of 15% and fees of 1.211%; bonds are expected to return 6.5% with a standard deviation of 5% and fees of 0.725%. Portfolios are rebalanced monthly, and withdrawals are made monthly. This example does not take into account taxes or required minimum distributions from retirement plans.

Figure 6: T. Rowe Price Dismal Decade Study

Make sure you understand the dynamic. The market is claimed to have an average rate of return of over 8%. In fact, if you read the fine print above, the assumption is a 10% rate of return for the S&P 500 with fees of around 1.2% Bonds are expected to return 6.5%. Yet the plan to withdraw just 4% with a 3% annual inflation adjustment ends up with only a 43% chance of success!

That isn't the worst of it. What really got to me was the response from T. Rowe Price when it released the study. In the words of Christine Fahlund, a senior financial planner at TRP,

> The belt-tightening option produced the best long-term result; by the end of 2010, the retiree's odds of

maintaining withdrawals up to age 95 (the remainder of the retirement period) jumped to 84 percent. "This really boils down to cutting back on what you withdraw -- but not everyone can stomach that big of a cut. So, the next best thing is not to increase your withdrawal amounts for inflation. Many of us think it's impossible to cut our spending, but the truth is we live in such affluence that we can cut if we absolutely have to.[14]

From a January 2013 Morningstar-sponsored study named, "Low Bond Yields and Safe Portfolio Withdrawal Rates":

> We find a retiree who wants a 90% probability of achieving a retirement income goal with a 30-year time horizon and a 40% equity portfolio would only have an initial withdrawal rate of 2.8%. Such a low withdrawal rate would require 42.9% more savings if the retiree wanted to pull the same dollar value out of the portfolio annually as he or she would get with a 4% withdrawal rate from a smaller portfolio.[15]

---

[14] Miller, Mark, "Lessons for retirees from the bear market decade," Reuters Money, February 16, 2011

[15] Morningstar Investment Management, January 21, 2013, *Low Bond Yields and Safe Portfolio Withdrawal Rates*, authored by David Blanchett, CFA, CFP®, Head of Retirement Research, Morningstar Investment Management; Michael Finke, Ph.D., CFP®, Professor and Ph.D. Coordinator at the Department of

So the 4% Rule is now the 2.8% Rule.

Why does this happen? It's because of a phenomenon we call "reverse dollar cost averaging." To get an idea about how this works, think back on how you were taught to save. Remember you were told to put aside the same amount every week or month and buy the same funds each time over a long period of time. The notion was that you would by some shares at a lower price, some higher, and some in between. In the end it would even out, and the amount you had saved would have most efficiently leveraged the gains in the markets over time. We call this "dollar cost averaging."

And it works pretty well, when you are saving. What they won't tell you is that it works even better when you are spending...but in reverse! Hence the name, "Reverse Dollar Cost Averaging."

Here's a simple illustration. Imagine that $500,000 we discussed earlier was made up of 10,000 shares at $50 each. And imagine that you will be taking 4% per year, or $20,000 in income. Translated into shares, that means you will be selling 400 shares a year. If you are doing the math, 400 shares a year times 30 is 12,000 shares, so we are already short by 2,000 shares. But no worries, your risky planner tells you, you are going to get gains of 8% a year! (If he's so confident, why can't you take 8% a year?)

Personal Financial Planning at Texas Tech University; Wade D. Pfau, Ph.D., CFA, Professor of Retirement Income at the American College

So armed with this wisdom of the ages you elected to retire in 2000. That year, you sell 400 shares, just as planned. Next year the market goes down by 2.1%, so in order to receive the original $20,000, you need to sell 408.33 shares. But you also budgeted for a 3% COLA, which means you need to sell 420.58 shares. Each year you have to sell more and more shares just to keep up. Below is a chart showing 4% a year beginning 1/1/2000:

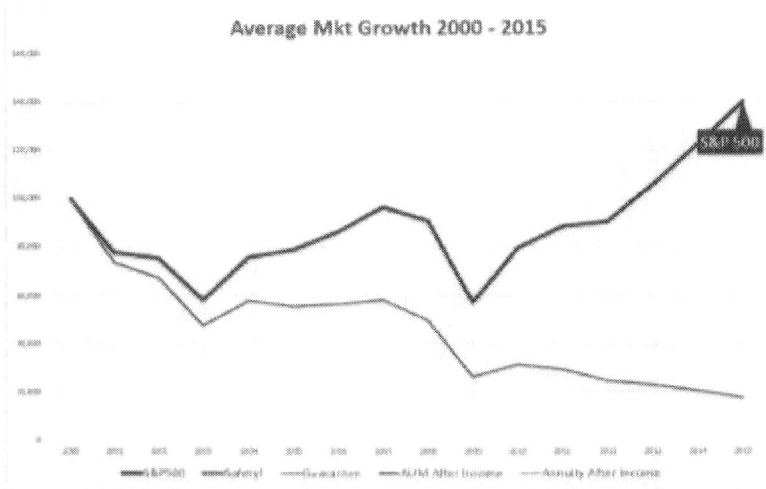

Figure 7: Results of 4% Rule assuming retirement in January 2000. Over 80% depleted after just 15 years.

It turns out that rates of return have very little to do with income planning success. Rather it's sequence of returns that determine success. Should you be lucky enough to have any down years come late in your retirement, chances are much greater that you won't run out of money. However, should those very same negative returns come early, they can do a significant amount of damage.

Nowhere in any of this is there mention of the fact that you *can* get a guaranteed lifetime income payout, much greater than the 4% touted by Wall Street, without ever running out of money. Let me say that again. It is possible to get much more than 4% – 50% or even more – from your retirement savings, *without running the risk of running out of money. Ever.* But they never, ever mention it. In fact when it does come up, they attack the idea as it if were from the Devil himself.

The trick, of course, is twofold. First you have to remove that whole when are you going to die thing. Nothing can reduce risk in a retirement plan or shore up your income and confidence in it like nailing down how long you need to plan for.

The second thing you need to do is find another risk class. In the market, there is only one risk class…the market itself. And while the market used to be based largely on things like PE ratios Today, however, it is so overvalued that these fundamentals seem to no longer apply. What is driving the market is the market itself. Computerize trading, derivatives, put and calls, margin trading, arbitrage. These are the fundamentals of today's market. It gambling, pure and simple, driven almost entirely by investor behavior. And that is not a risk class that can be counted on, as will be seen in the next section.

"Thinking something does not make it true. Wanting something does not make it real." — Michelle Hodkin

Big Secret #5: Most investors get much less than the market average.

The whole premise of market returns presumes you have the intestinal fortitude to ride out long bear markets. The average investor actually gets much less in the market because people tend to be motivated more by emotions than logic when it comes to markets. So they tend to get out after long downturns and get back in after rallies have been in place for a while.

In fact, according to Dalbar's Quantitative Analysis of Investor Behavior:

> For the 20 years ended December 31, 2008, equity, fixed income and asset allocation fund investors had

average annual returns of 1.87%, 0.77% and 1.67%, respectively.[16]

And, from the May/June 2009 Journal of Indexes:

> For the past forty years, ordinary long-term treasury bonds have outpaced investing in the stock market, which means the only 'rewards' investors have received for taking the extra risk of stocks and equity mutual funds are sleepless nights and broken retirement dreams.[17]

But it's different now, right? This raging bull we've been having has got to have settled people down? Why not show us a more current study?

Okay, here it is. The results of Dalbar's 2014 study:

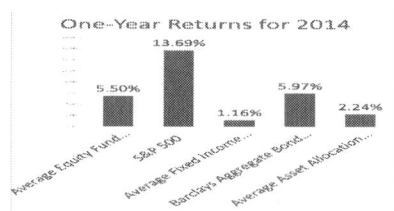

Figure 8: Dalbar's One Year Returns, 2014

---

[16] March 9, 2009, DALBAR's Quantitative Analysis of Investor Behavior (QAIB)
[17] Arnot, Robert: "Bonds, Why Bother?" Journal of Indexes, May/June 2009

Note this is just a single year of returns. All a savvy investor would have needed to do is stay the course in the S&P 500 in 2014. Yet the average fund investor got almost 60% less than one who would have been steady in an index fund.

Why does this happen? According to Jay Mooreland on The Emotional Investor website, May 11, 2015 (emphasis his):

> There are lots of reasons why investors perform poorly, but the bottom line is that many investors are incapable of actually investing. Rather, they cross that fine line from investing and into speculating. *Investors tend to be more concerned with the price movements of the underlying security than in the enterprise value of the company.* This is demonstrated by the average mutual fund retention rate.

So we seem to be our worst enemy. We can't get the promised rates of return because we can't tolerate the risk associated with – the very activity – that produces those returns. We are creatures, after all, of emotion, in this case fear and greed, which cause us to make very bad decisions in the face of very confusing situations.

Why is that? Well, first, these are primal instincts that have served us well since sabre-tooth tigers were circling our campfires. So it's hard to resist them. But isn't there more? Isn't there that niggling but persistent little feeling that maybe something we don't quite comprehend is going on? Something we can't quite touch?

Something that if we were made aware of might explain a lot? Something that Wall Street does everything it can to hide?

What it, for example, the average rates of return that are constantly being touted were all just a big lie. Might that do it?

"Unthinking respect for authority is the greatest enemy of truth."
— Albert Einstein

Big Secret #4: Average rates of return lie

Well, as it happens, secret number six that Wall Street doesn't want you to know is (are you ready for it?) *average rates of return are misleading to the point of being meaningless.*

Here's an example. Assume you have $100,000 and the market goes up by 10% next year. How much money do you have?

"Easy," you say: "$110,000."

$$\$100{,}000 \times 1.1 = \$110{,}000$$

"Right," I say. "So what's yer point?" you say.

Okay, stay with me for a moment. Assume the next year it goes down 10%. How much do you have now?

"Easy," you say, poking me in the eye: "$100,000."

+10% - 10% = 0. $100,000 x 1.0 = $100,000

"Not so fast," I say, blinking rapidly.

$110,000 x .90 = $99,000, not $100,000!

See, when markets go up, the gain is added to your principal. You don't get the calculated gain plus a corresponding growth of principal (huh?).

But when markets go down, both your gain and your principal are both attacked (I know...bad English. But I'm making a point, okay?) So a 10% loss is always more impactful than a 10% gain, even though the average rate of return is zero, the real rate of return is something else.

+10% - 10% = 0.

Removing risk is much more important than increasing gains.

Here's an example I like to go over during my financial planning workshops. The following graph shows the Dow from 1929 to the end of 2012. The average rate of return during this period of time was 6.72% (not anywhere near the 8% risky planners like to tout!).

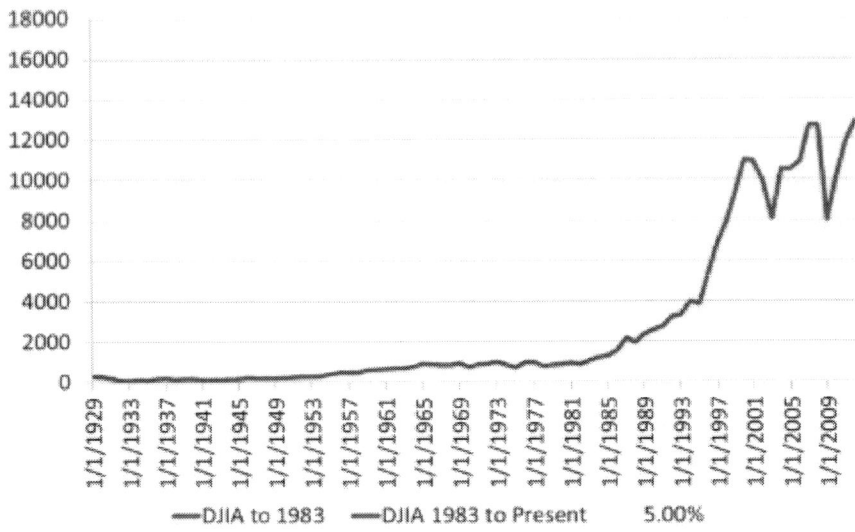

Figure 9: Dow Jones Industrial Average 1983-2010

"But hey, 6.72% is nothing to scoff at, right? And there isn't anything better than the markets for savings. So I feel pretty good," you say, poking me in the eye, yet again.

Ducking, I say again, "Wait a minute. What if you could have gotten a safe, compound interest rate of say, 5% during that period of time?"

"Five percent?" you scoff. I got almost two percentage points higher. How can five percent possibly compete?"

Let's take a look. Here's a chart showing five percent rate of return during that same period, compounded with no risk:

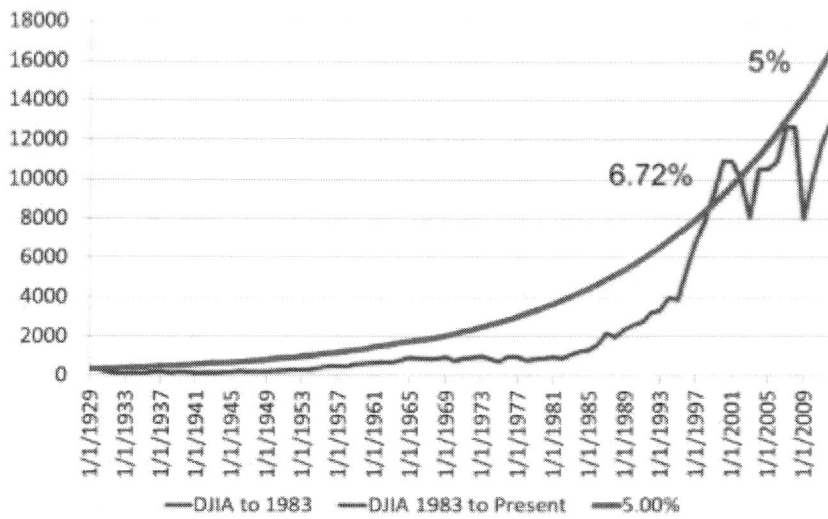

Figure 10: Dow Jones Industrial Average vs. 5% Fixed Growth 1983-2010

Again, this is a function of the principle outlined in the previous section about rates of return. When you can eliminate risk you get a much, much better result, even if your overall rate of return is lower. And, going back to the Reverse Dollar Cost Averaging principle, since you never sustain a loss, you never have to sell distressed shares, meaning your money has more chance of lasting as long as you do.

To reiterate: safety is the most important single element you can introduce into your portfolio to ensure that you have enough money to live out your life. It makes sense, doesn't it? If you were coming up short on your monthly bills, would you take your life savings to Vegas? Think about it. And if you were employing a financial planner who recommended taking your savings to Vegas, what would you think?

So why then are you so sanguine about having all your money in the market? How in the world does that make any kind of sense? It doesn't. And you know it. And your parents knew it. And their parents knew it. That's why for so many years people relied on safe assets for their retirement. Assets like Treasuries, CDs, pensions, income annuities, etc. These were the stuff of retirement, not risky market assets.

Safety. It's the most important element of retirement income planning. And that brings us to…

"It ain't what we don't know that gets us in trouble, it's what we know for certain that just ain't so." — Mark Twain

Big Secret #3: Bonds are not a safe alternative.

For decades people have been sold on the idea that bonds are safe, and that a diversified portfolio of stocks and bonds will provide the necessary safety along with growth that you need to achieve the retirement of your dreams. This was considered gospel. It was unshakeable truth.

Unshakeable, that is, until 2008. So let me ask you; have you ever known anyone who lost money in bonds? Most people will say yes to this question. In fact most people who had bonds during the meltdown of 2008 lost a substantial portion of their savings whether they were in bonds or stocks.

The truth is, bonds are not safe. Somehow they got branded safe because they have a fixed income component. You buy a $1,000 bond at five percent and you know you are going to get that $50 a year as long as you hold the bond, unless, of course the company goes out of business, and then you are in the same boat as all the other creditors. Or, unless interest rates go down and your bonds are called! (Hard to catch a break, here, isn't it!)

See, that's the point. As a bond holder you are just a creditor, and if you hold a debenture bond, an unsecured creditor. And companies go out of business, and so do municipalities. Remember Enron? How about Orange County? Detroit? Fresno? I lived in Orange County when it declared bankruptcy, when one of the richest counties in the nation defaulted on its bondholders.

Not only are you a creditor, but a bond is a security (I never understood why the call these things securities; I think they should be called "riskies"). And the values of securities go up and down with supply and demand.

Here are some troubling facts about bonds. Today there is about two and one-half times as much money being held in bonds as there is in equities. That's a huge number; nearly $100 trillion. That's trillion, with a "tr"! What would happen to the economy, and your retirement, if that huge bubble popped? And how likely is that to happen?

Bond prices fluctuate with interest rates. As interest rates go up, bond prices go down, and vice versa. Here's how that works.

Assume you buy the afore-mentioned $1,000 bond (that's how bonds are sold), with a face value of 5%. That means every year you are going to get $50 in interest for as long as you hold the bond. And, if you hold the bond to maturity, and the company is still in business, you will get your $1,000 back.

Now assume interest rates go up to 10%. What happens to the value of your bond? Again, if you hold it to maturity, nothing. You will get your full $1,000 back.

But in the bond market, your bond's value has gone down by 50%! That's because no one is going to pay full price for a bond that is only paying 5% in a 10% interest rate environment. Would you? If brand spankin' new bonds were being sold with an interest rate of 10%, would you pay full price for one paying only five? Of course not. If you were going to purchase the 5% bond, what would you pay?

$$5/10 \times 1,000 = 500$$

So suddenly your once very valuable bond has gone down in value by 50%. Now of course you can elect to hold it to maturity, and if the company is still in business you will get your money back. But that does mean that you are willing to continue to accept a 5% interest rate in a 10% environment. This may be okay, but it certainly is something to consider. And if you are at all concerned about the value of your holdings, it bears a great deal of scrutiny.

Now, it's important to consider the following question; and remember we have record amounts of money in bonds...

Are interest rates likely to go up, or go down in the future? In order to answer, take a look at the following interest rate chart, courtesy of MoneyCafe.com from data provided by the Federal Reserve:

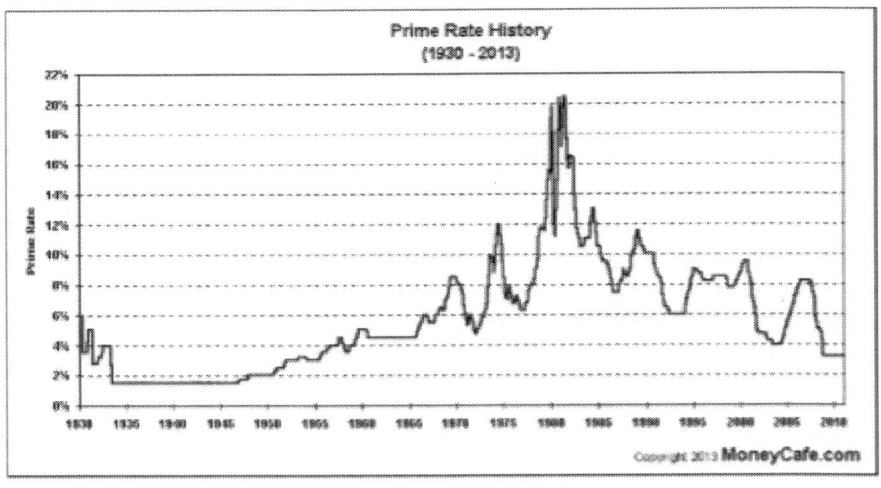

Figure 11: Prime Rate History 1930-2013

On the above historical prime rate chart note that the prime interest rate is lower now than it has been at any time since

1953. That's 60 years! Longer than many of us have been alive. And it's being held at this low rate by the Federal Reserve, which is buying up $85 billion (with a B!) worth of our debt per month.

So ask yourself. What happens when the Fed stops buying the debt? Are interest rates going to go up? Are bonds going to crash? And if they do...if $100 trillion suddenly takes a nosedive, what happens to the rest of the economy? What happens to your stock holdings? Do you really want to find out?

"The more I see, the less I know for sure." — John Lennon

Big Secret #2: The only guarantees on variable annuities are the fees you will pay

More often than I would like, I meet people whose advisors sold them a variable annuity as a "safe haven" and "guaranteed" place to grow their money. This is not usually a good thing for the client, so why are they the number one annuity sold by the planning industry?

Most planners are stock brokers, and are constrained by what their broker/dealers permit them to sell (remember the discussion about fiduciaries at the beginning of this book). Most broker/dealers do not either understand, like, or deal in fixed or indexed products...they are in the securities business. Remember, to a hammer salesman, everything looks like a nail.

Now you should know that everyone in the investment community just LOVES variable annuities. Brokers love them because they carry high commissions and often ongoing fees.

Wire houses (the Merrill Lynches or Ameriprises of the world) love them because once you are in them you are stuck by surrender charges and fees. Like in 401(k)s, big investment firms pay a fee to be included in the mix. Once done, they have a captive customer who is subject to surrender terms and charges. They get to charge you their normal, and in many cases, much higher, fees than in other assets and funds…you are captive, and subject to a penalty for early termination, after all.

Insurance companies love them because they get to charge high fees, trap you into long-term contracts, and they are not responsible for keeping your money safe like they are in fixed annuities, since with a VA your money is in the market, and you, not they, take all the risk. Insurance companies LOVE this.

Getting the picture?

Further, the fees charged on variable annuities can be very high and are often for unnecessary and unwanted features. Here's an example of the fees associated with a typical variable annuity taken right off a Morningstar report.

Base Contract Charges				Fee		Cost	
Mortality & Expense (M&E)				1.50%		$	1,500.00
Admin				0.30%		$	300.00
Contract Fee				0.00%		$	-
Distribution Charge				0.25%		$	250.00
Total Annual Charges				2.05%		$	2,050.00
Sub-Account Expenses	Mgt. Fee	Other Exp	12b-1	Total Exp	Allocations		Charge
JHVIT	0.30%	0.03%	0.75%	1.08%	$ 12,000.00	$	129.60
JHVIT II	0.49%	0.06%	0.75%	1.30%	$ 13,500.00	$	175.50
JHVIT III	0.78%	0.03%	0.25%	1.06%	$ 14,900.00	$	157.94
JHVIT IV	0.92%	0.07%	0.25%	1.24%	$ 12,000.00	$	148.80
JHVIT IV	0.92%	0.07%	0.25%	1.24%	$ 12,000.00	$	148.80
JHVIT IV	0.92%	0.07%	0.25%	1.24%	$ 12,000.00	$	148.80
JHVIT V	0.78%	0.04%	0.25%	1.07%	$ 23,600.00	$	252.52
Effective Charges				1.16%	$ 100,000.00	$	1,161.96
Riders				Fee		Cost	
Income Rider #1				0.50%		$	500.00
Death Benefit Rider #1				0.79%		$	790.00
Additional Riders				0.00%		$	-
				0.00%		$	-
				0.00%		$	-
				0.00%		$	-
Total Annual Rider Charges				1.29%		$	790.00
Total Charges							
Base Contract Expenses				2.05%		$	2,050.00
Rider Expenses				1.29%		$	790.00
Sub-Account Expenses				1.16%		$	1,161.96
Total Charges				4.50%		$	4,001.96

Figure 12: Morningstar Variable Annuity Fee Report

What are these fees and what do you get for them? First are the "base contract charges." These are the fees charged by the insurance company for putting the contract together and making it available. Not for managing your money or anything else, just putting it together and administering the paperwork. Looking closely, you can see that this totally superfluous activity costs you 2%. In other words, if you had a VA for, say, $250,000 and held if for 10 years, the insurance company would charge you $50,000 in fees! For what? What do they provide that's worth 20% of the value of what you put in?

Next you have the subaccount expenses. These are the expenses charged by the fund managers. Remember, variable annuities are basically a limited number of mutual funds wrapped in an insurance contract. So far you are in for 3.31% just for base charges. On our $250,000 annuity above, that's now $82,750 skimmed off the top. What do these charges buy you? Are you any safer being in the annuity than you would be in the market? Not at all. In fact you are much less safe as you have had an automatic drain of $82,750 whether you make money or lose money.

What about the riders? The argument could be made that the reason you took out this contract was to have access to the riders. So let's look at how those work. Often there is a lot of confusion about these riders and they are also often misrepresented when they are sold.

This particular contract has two of the most common riders; the guaranteed withdrawal income rider and the guaranteed death benefit rider. This latter one is my favorite because it shows just how lousy these contracts can be.

Here's how it works. The rider guarantees your beneficiary will never receive less than your original amount of premium, less any withdrawals, should you die. The cost of this rider is in this case .79% of the greater of the contract value or original premium. In other words, on a $100,000 deposit, it can never be less than $790, but it can be more (an egregious charge, as we will see in a moment). So, let's run through the various scenarios.

First, assume the market goes down, by say, 10% and the owner dies. What exactly are you getting for the $790 a year you are paying? Remember, the rider merely guarantees you will not receive less than you put in. So the benefit received will be:

$$\$100k - \$90k = \$10k$$

So, you are effectively paying $790 a year for $10,000 in life insurance protection (sometimes). But wait! There's more!

Assume the market bounces back and you are even when the owner dies. What is the benefit you are getting for your $790 a year?

$$\$100k - \$100k = \$0$$

Right! $790 a year with no benefit at all. But again, there's more!

Assume the market has gone up fairly dramatically since the annuity was purchases, and its value is $150k when the owner dies.

What's the benefit now?

$$\$100k - \$150k = -\$50k = \$0$$

So again, it's zero. No benefit. But this is where it really gets good from the insurance company's standpoint. Remember the cost of the rider was .79% of the greater of (that egregious charge) the premium paid or contract value? So now the cost of this rider that isn't buying you any benefit at all is

$$.79\% \times \$150k = \$1,185$$

Right! As the insurance company's exposure goes down, the cost goes up! I only wish I could get into a business like this. Oh, wait...I am! I just don't quite have the chutzpah to sell these things to my clients.

So you are now in to the tune of $102,500 over a ten year period on your $250,000 annuity. Again, I ask, what have you received for it?

Now let's look at the other rider...the minimum income withdrawal benefit. This is another favorite of mine, for a different reason entirely. Unlike the death benefit rider which has no good purpose whatsoever (a 62 year-old in medium good health can buy a 20-year term life policy for $100k for just $654.60, and the premium and death benefit both stay steady for a full 20 years), this income rider can have some benefit. The problem is it's almost always sold in a misleading fashion.

I frequently have people come into my office with a variable annuity and they will tell me it has a 5% or 6% minimum guaranteed return. Invariably they are referring to the roll-up amount of the income rider, and this is not the same as a guaranteed rate of return. Let me explain.

Income riders, which we will discuss in detail a bit later in this book, do serve a purpose, which is to guarantee income. So the guaranteed rate of return agents and stock brokers are selling their clients in the case of a VA is not a guaranteed minimum 5% that can be earned and cashed in at the end of the contract. It's a pretend number that is only used to calculate income from the income rider.

It works like this. If the contract starts at $100,000 and is held for 10 years, the income rider is guaranteed to grow at a minimum rate of 5%. That means its value will be at least $162,889. But it isn't your money. It's an income base. That means it's only used to calculate income in conjunction with an age factor.

So now assume the owner was 55 when the annuity was purchased, and 65 when income is to start. A typical age factor would be somewhere around 4% for a 65 year-old. Therefore income would be derived as:

$$\$162,889 \times .04 = \$6,515$$

That's it. That's all it does. It provides a number from which to calculate an income amount.

All told, your $250,000 annuity has cost you, at a minimum, $115,000 over a ten year period. Guaranteed. And remember, that's a minimum amount. If you make no money (although in fairness, it could be less if you lose money…but not much). Annuity fees are based on the value of the annuity. So, if you are lucky and the annuity contract goes up by, say, 5% a year (requiring 9.6% because of everyone's fingers in the pie), your "partners" would receive $163,378. Guaranteed!

Here is a quote from Jane Bryant Quinn on variable annuities:

> You rarely find me so deeply angry at a common investment product that I dream of blowing it to smithereens….. My target: tax-deferred, variable annuities.[18]

And, from John Biggs, former chair of TIAA-CREF pension funds which invented variable annuities:

> I cannot imagine a personal financial situation where I'd recommend a VA (variable annuity) as a good idea.[19]

---

[18] Jane Bryant Quinn, "One Faulty Investment," Newsweek, August 30, 2006.
[19] Ibid

In a nutshell, our objections to variable annuities are:

- High risk
- High fees
- High surrender charges
- Limited investment options
- Long surrender periods

Basically, if you are interested in risk and fees, go directly into the market...your options are greater, you have no surrender charges or periods, and fees are generally much, much (much, much, much!) lower.

"A lie can run around the world before the truth can get its boots on." — James Watt

Big Secret #1: The very best thing for income planning is annuities

"*Now waitaminnut*," I can almost hear you shouting. "Didn't you just spend the whole last section ***trashing*** annuities? And now you want me to believe they are the best things for income?"

Well, yes. That's it. But not a variable annuity where you take all the risk and pay out exorbitant (immoral?) fees. Here we are talking about fixed annuities where the insurance company takes the risk. And not just any fixed annuity, a hybrid fixed annuity.

"I *knew* it," you say. "I *just knew* this whole book thing was just a scam to trick me into buying an annuity! My broker was right! You can't trust anyone!"

Okay, just for a moment, let's say that's true. Let's stipulate our whole goal here is to sneak up on you and foist an annuity on you while you're not looking...instead of, say, an oil shale partnership. What would end up happening? You might:

- Create a *personal pension plan* you can never outlive.
- Receive *market-like returns* with no (zero, zip, nada) risk to your principal and accrued interest.
- Ensure guaranteed income for the rest of your life at a higher rate than with any other investment—without giving up control of your money.
- *Reduce taxes* on your investment savings to under 2%.
- *Reduce or eliminate the taxes* you pay on your Social Security benefits.
- Completely *remove your IRA/401(k) from your estate*, passing 100% of your beginning balance to your heirs, *tax free* while enjoying greater income than provided by your RMD.
- Provide all of these benefits (and more) with *low or no fees or risk*.

Higher payouts, lower taxes, low, or no fees, no risk and solid guarantees. What's so bad about all that?

What Makes Them So Good?

One simple thing. The big secret. The thing you can't do with any other type of asset class or investment vehicle. The thing that is so threatening to Wall Street that in 2008 when the entire economy was melting down and Bernie Madoff and other Wall Street crooks were robbing us blind, it was the only thing the SEC was actually concerned about.

It's the truth. So much money had been flowing out of the market into safe-money hybrid annuities (a.k.a. fixed index annuities, or FIAs), the SEC attempted a takeover of FIA regulations from the insurance industry so that it could kill them. And its reasoning? DANGER! FIAs were dangerous to people who bought them. You see, they didn't protect investors from **UPSIDE RISK!** Here is the actual wording from the actual ruling:

> Thus, the protections provided…may not adequately transfer investment risk from the purchaser to the insurer when amounts payable by an insurer under the contract <u>are more likely than not to exceed</u> the amounts guaranteed under the contract…[20]

---

[20] U.S. SEC Ruling about FIAs under 151-a 73 Federal Register 37752, July 1, 2008

Yup, you read it right. The SEC wanted to protect you from the possibility **that you might make more money than the contract guarantees.** Excess profits...a terrible thing (unless you are, ahem, actually a Wall Street maven!) Really. You can't make this stuff up!

Now Congress and the courts saw through what the SEC was trying to do, so they stepped in and stopped it. So Wall Street couldn't kill the things. What was next? Here's an excerpt from an article in Life Health Pro, January 2, 2012, by a very well-known annuity expert, Jack Marrion:

> In one recent weekly issue of *Investment News* there were three articles on fixed annuities—this from a periodical that in the past might have mentioned fixed annuities three times in a year. One of the articles was titled 'Wirehouses Warming to Indexed Annuities,' centering on how wirehouses are now embracing them. As a Merrill Lynch managing director said, 'Five years ago, nobody hated the product more than me, but now I've seen the light.' Wall Street has discovered index annuities. Why now? They say it's because the products have changed and are no longer 'bad' but that's not the real reason. Wall Street

is looking at index annuities they failed to kill them and their traditional solutions aren't working well…

As index annuity sales grew after the millennium bear market, Wall Street and its minions bombarded securities regulators with exaggerated stories of index annuity sales abuses and how agents needed to be stopped. In truth, there were sales abuses, but never even close to the extent that the naysayers proclaimed. Because the annuity industry remained silent and let the securities industry write the story the media was full of tales—actually a few tales repeated nauseam—of how bad index annuities were. The result was Rule 151A, which would have killed index annuities. However, the annuity industry finally rallied and managed to kill the rule instead; meaning index annuities would still be competing for consumer dollars. [21]

So what's this big number one top secret? The biggest thing that insurance and annuities do better than anything else? The

---

[21] Marrion, Jack. *Life Health Pro* 2 Jan. 2012.

thing that was so threatening to Wall Street that the SEC felt compelled to nuke them out of existence (because, as you will recall, there was not enough UPSIDE protection!)?

They eliminate and spread the risk. They take it off you and put it on a giant pool of people. Just like insurance companies do with car insurance, or home insurance or health insurance.

This is huge. This is the very most important thing you can do when it comes to planning for your income, as you will see.

Let's look at this from the inside out. Insurance companies use something called actuarial science, or the "Law of Large Numbers," to predict how often things will happen by studying and measuring events and causes in large population groups. These events might be automobile crashes, fires, sickness, disability, death, or even not dying.

This is a huge advantage; so huge in fact that it is generally accepted that no one can possibly self-insure in most areas of life. In nearly every area of life, home owners, health, automobile, disability, flood, death, liability and many others, it is generally accepted that purchasing insurance and spreading the risk is the safe, prudent and accepted way to go...*except in retirement and long term care!*

Somehow in these areas it is "too expensive," "too exotic," "too dangerous," too anything they can think of to use the most tested, safest and conservative method of achieving security: spreading the risk. No, much better to take all of your savings and put it into the most dangerous and risky place possible, like shale oil or a market that is subject to the whims of weather, governments, terrorist attacks, interest rate spikes, massive short selling and arbitrage, and even little city-states like Cypress…and the SEC and Wall Street community call this "prudent."

And the thing is, spreading the risk is so much more valuable than a point…two points…even five or six points in return. And it's tax free, completely safe and largely free of fees.

If I, as an income planner, am asked to create a plan for you, an individual (or couple if you are married), I have a very small pool of people to work with. And since most likely we have no idea how long you are going to live (that when are you going to die thing again!), I have to plan on you living as long as is possible (or likely possible). Now today life expectancies have risen dramatically and they continue to rise. In fact, the older you are, the longer you are expected to live.

Statistically, if you are married and age 65, there is a greater than 50% chance that one of you will live to age 93. That's nearly a 30 year planning horizon.

So assume you have $500,000 saved up for your retirement. Now, as a prudent planner, I would want to be sure that you had enough money to last the whole 30 years. So, not knowing what kind of rate of return you could get, I could simply divide 500,000 by 30 and advise you to take no more than $16,667 per year, or about 3.3%, thereby guaranteeing you have enough money for the rest of your life. Good, but not great. In line, not so coincidentally, with Morningstar's "2.8% Rule," but actually a lot safer.

Let's try another way. If you are currently 65 years old and male, your life expectancy is right around 80. If female it's about 82. Now it's important to understand the term, "life expectancy." All it means is that by the time you reach 80 or 82, half the people who were 65 at the same time you were are now dead. Half of them are still alive. Further, if you are one of the lucky ones still living, your life expectancy is now around 88. And if you live to 88 it goes into the 90s. So the longer you live, the longer you can *expect* to live.

So, at age 82, half the people are dead, but half are still alive. Which half do you plan to be in? Do you think you will be lucky enough to live past 82, or do you think you will die sooner? If you knew, it might make a difference in how you plan, right?

But, as Yogi Berra once said, "It's very difficult to make predictions, especially about the future." So, as outlined above, the prudent planner would plan for a long life expectancy. But at what cost?

If you went back to that $500,000 example mentioned above, and were able to plan for just 15-17 years, it could make quite a difference in your lifestyle, couldn't it.

After all, $500,000 divided by 17 is $29,412 a year. FYI, that's 5.9% a year. That's a lot more than the $16,667 we initially discussed for 30 years, and more even than the $20,000 annually that the Monte Carlo plan provides, and certainly more than the $14,000 provided by Morningstar's 2.8% Rule. Since we don't need a rate of return, it's 100% guaranteed...just put it in a CD or T-Bill or some other safe money vehicle and it will be there every year like clockwork when you need it...until age 82.

Just plan for life expectancy and everything is great...unless you are one of the "lucky" ones who live longer. So, what to do? Plan for the long life and reduce your payout to $16,667, or take your chances with more in the Monte Carlo plan?

Okay, there are your choices. Bet on life expectancy and spend 5.9% a year, or hedge your bets and take only 2.8%, which is less than half. You decide. Choose. Because if you are going to use a traditional Wall Street (risky) approach, those are about your choices. Or you can purchase a variable annuity, whereby your advisors get the 5% and you still have to settle for less.

We know that of the people who plan in the traditional manner, 40% plan for too short a life span and run out of money too soon and 40% plan for too long a life and die with more money than they need. Only about 20% actually get it right.

But what if you *could* plan for life expectancy? What if you could plan for life expectancy *and* a healthy rate of return? What if you could do that with exact precision, knowing exactly when you will die and how much money your investments will earn over time, without risk of loss? How much would that be worth to you? What if you could, after all, tell me when you're going to die?

How much would that be worth? If you are 65 and have $500,000 and could know all of those things, you could get around $27,500 for the rest of your life; guaranteed, no matter how long you live. And if there was money left over when you died it would all go to your designated beneficiaries.

How? It's called *insurance*, or in the case of income, *annuities*. It's the very same method used by all pension plans, state lotteries, Social Security, and every other planning mechanism that has to pay out money over a long period of time. And they get it right 100% of the time.

Wall Street hates this part

But it gets even better. If you know in advance that you are planning to retire at, say, age 70, and you are 60 years old and have that $500,000 we previously spoke about, you can dramatically increase the amount of your retirement payout by planning ahead.

Just like variable annuities, hybrid annuities have an income rider that allows the insurance company to not only calculate how much it will pay you in income if you start today, but how much income it will pay you later if you delay. Here's how it works.

You give the insurance company your money, and it invests it in very safe general fund accounts (the same accounts backing its life insurance policies) for a period of time...say 10 years. After that 10 year period the insurance company will guarantee you a payout based on the time it has had to manage your money and your age. In this case your income for two people at age 70 after waiting 10 years would be about $55,000. Guaranteed. For the rest of your life (*see* Figure 13: Income for Life Illustration). Note, also, you don't have to take income at 70. If you wanted income, at, say 65, it would be $35,039. The longer you wait, the more your annual income.

Income Age	GWIB Amt	Single Income	Dual Income	Income Amount	Estimated Account Balance	Required Amount (Monte Carlo)	Required Interest Rate (Monte Carlo)
61	589,600	26,532	23,584		569,250	884,400	61%
62	632,051	28,442	25,282		589,174	948,077	31%
63	677,559	30,490	27,102		609,795	1,016,338	23%
64	726,343	32,685	29,054		631,138	1,089,515	19%
65	778,640	38,932	35,039		653,227	1,297,733	19%
66	834,702	41,735	37,562		676,090	1,391,170	17%
67	894,000	44,740	40,266		699,754	1,491,334	15%
68	959,226	47,961	43,165		724,246	1,598,710	14%
69	1,028,290	51,415	46,273		749,594	1,713,817	13%
70	1,102,327	60,628	55,116	55,116	718,784	2,020,933	14%
71	1,181,695	64,993	59,085	55,116	686,896	2,166,440	13%
72	1,266,777	69,673	63,339	55,116	653,892	2,322,424	13%
73	1,357,985	74,689	67,899	55,116	619,733	2,489,638	12%
74	1,455,760	80,067	72,788	55,116	584,378	2,668,893	12%
75	1,560,574	93,634	85,832	55,116	547,786	3,121,149	12%
76	1,672,936	100,376	92,011	55,116	509,913	3,346,871	12%
77	1,793,387	107,603	98,636	55,116	470,714	3,586,774	12%
78	1,922,511	115,361	105,738	55,116	430,144	3,845,022	11%
79	2,060,932	123,656	113,351	55,116	388,153	4,121,864	11%
80	2,209,319	143,606	132,559	55,116	344,693	4,786,857	11%
81	2,209,319	143,606	132,559	55,116	299,712	4,786,857	11%
82	2,209,319	143,606	132,559	55,116	253,157	4,786,857	10%
83	2,209,319	143,606	132,559	55,116	204,972	4,786,857	10%
84	2,209,319	143,606	132,559	55,116	155,100	4,786,857	9%
85	2,209,319	154,662	143,606	55,116	103,483	5,156,077	9%
86	2,209,319	154,662	143,606	55,116	50,060	5,156,077	9%

Figure 13: Income for Life Illustration

Now, compare that amount to what you would have to make in the stock market to get the same amount of income with the same level of guarantees (good luck!).

First, you have determine what level of payout you want to receive. If you are content with the previously mentioned 4%, you will need to have $1,375,000 saved by age 70:

$$\$55,000/.04 = \$1,375,000$$

But we already know that is very iffy; after the last decade we only have about a 43% chance of success using Monte Carlo and the 4% Rule, and the annuity provides us with 100%. So what payout factor should we use to get a 100% chance of success?

Many Wall Street planners are now recommending that instead of using a 4% payout, that to be safe you should figure on about 2.5% to 3%. Get that. You have $500,000 socked away and your planner will only recommend you take out $15,000! Further, according to that Morningstar study, 2.8% only provides 90%. Taking any less, however, seems ridiculous, so we'll have to settle for that.

So using the 2.8% number, in order to get $55,000 a year in income at age 70, you would have to have the following.

$55,000/.028 = $1,964,285

So what rate of return do you need to get over the next 10 years to accumulate $1,964,285, starting with $500k?

According to the future value calculator on Investopedia.com, you would need to have a steady return of **14.66%**, every year for the next 10, net of fees, to reach your savings goal. How likely is that?

Why is all this so important? Simple, because it lets one actually make a plan. We have a saying: "Until you remove risk, it's not planning, it's hoping." And we are planners, not hopers. If I create a plan, I will write it down, on paper, and give it to you. That to me represents my reputation and my integrity. In addition to yours, it represents my future and the security of my family. So if I write something down and give it to you I want to have a pretty good idea I can actually deliver it.

These Are Not Your Father's Annuities

You should know that 90% of the time when brokers, TV and radio commentators, magazines and newspapers, etc., mention annuities, they are either talking about VAs or immediate annuities. We have already discussed VAs, but haven't mentioned immediate annuities, a.k.a. Single Premium Immediate Annuities, or SPIAs. These were the traditional annuities that required you to give up control of your money in return for a lifetime payout. A friend of mine who is also in this business calls this committing "annuicide."

The market has changed dramatically since the 1990s and the insurance industry has caught up in a big way. The primary differences between now and then has to do with the way the new generation of retirees and pre-retirees think of their money.

Our parents were brought up on the idea of the defined benefits plan, or pension. It was based on the idea that they contributed during their working lives and when they retired they got a specific benefit...pension, healthcare, etc., for the rest of their lives. They really never related to the pool of money funding it; they were more concerned about the ongoing security they received. For them, a SPIA would have been just dandy. In fact, my father had one. He very happily spent the insurance company's money until the ripe old age of 91, secure in the knowledge it would be there each and every month, 100% of the time, with an iron-clad contractual guarantee.

In contrast, our generation was brought up on the modern 401(k) which began in 1980 and shifted the risk, and burden of management, onto the retiree (that be you!). Instead of watching the end game...or the benefits, we were taught to keep our eye on the pool of money being accumulated.

If you think about it, this is entirely backwards and counter-productive to our best interests. After all, what are you putting the money aside for? Is it so you can admire the size of your nest egg, or is it to provide the best, most abundant and secure retirement you can possibly have? So whose interests were served by this new paradigm? Who wins in this scenario? You, who are put in a positon of counting pennies your entire life, even after amassing more than you could have ever imagined? Or Wall Street and its agents who get to manage the money and skim 3% to 6% off the top, for decades and decades? You tell me?

Anyway, back to the point. The old fashioned annuity that concentrated on lifetime payouts and benefits through annuitization no longer fit the model. We now needed a newer model that allowed people to keep control of their money *and* get a meaningful lifetime payout. So the industry came up with a whole new line of policies that met both needs: the need to keep control of one's money, and the need for excellent and safe returns and guaranteed lifetime income streams that could only be provided by an insured retirement plan.

Enter the modern Fixed Index Annuity. We call it the "have your cake and eat it, too" annuity, or the hybrid annuity. Try this on for size:

It's completely, 100% safe. You cannot lose a dime of your principal or any accrued interest unless you pull your money out before the surrender period is over.

Okay, now wait a minute. Weren't surrender periods and charges one of the main reasons you objected to variable annuities a little earlier? Yes, they were. And here's why…they didn't buy you anything (except the privilege of paying exorbitant and immoral fees)! Hold on and I will explain. In the meantime, back to the advantages of the FIA:

- They allow you to receive market-like gains without market risk (see the section on eliminating market risk).
- They provide superior, guaranteed, lifetime income without giving up control of your money.
- You pay no fees or commissions out of your money (unless you add certain benefits, and then you pay a SMALL, clearly stated fee with a clear understanding of the benefits received).
- They have excellent liquidity: you can always have access up to 10% (or sometimes more) of your money per year with ZERO surrender charges. If you need more, we have others that provide up to 100% of your principal with no penalties to principal; only interest. If you die, end up in a nursing home or become terminally ill, the whole amount is paid out without penalty.
- They provide huge tax advantages.

Okay, now back to our point about surrender periods. Unless fees and surrender charges are buying you something they are not good. With a hybrid annuity, the surrender charge is buying you something. It's buying complete safety, market participation without the risk, minimal or no fees, lifetime income without giving up control of your money and huge tax advantages. With the exception of the last item, none of these things is available with the VA, and yet you still have surrender charges and those exorbitant fees. So that's why we don't like them.

Protection from Stock Market Losses

One of the main issues today's retirees have is losses in the market. Indeed, many have called the first decade of the 21st Century the "Lost Decade." If you had held your money just in the S&P 500 from January 1, 2001 until the end of 2010, you would have averaged a −3.1% average return on your money, for a LOSS of 31% over that 10 year period! That is not supposed to happen in long-term stock market investing!

But with the markets at all-time highs, isn't this all moot? Well, think of it this way. On January 3, 2000 the Dow Jones closed at 11,357. At today's close (October 2015), it closed at 17,663; a near-record high. That means in the ensuing 15 year period you had an annual return of 2.99% per year! Now net your fees out of that.

But somehow people never believe me when I show them these figures...after all it goes against everything they "know." One of my favorite sayings is by the slave Jim in Huck Finn: "It ain't what we don't know that gives us trouble, it's what we know for certain that just ain't so."

Ben Franklin is reputed to have once said (so is Einstein, and Thomas Jefferson, and I believe, Kermit the Frog…heck, I say it all the time!), "The definition of insanity is doing the same thing over and over again and expecting different results." It doesn't really matter who said it, it bears reflection. Ask yourself, does this apply to the way you manage your money? For many people it does. They know what they are doing isn't working. They know they are riding a bubble that will burst. They've seen it happen over and over and over, but they are so caught up in fear that they just keep on doing it. And by way of "comforting" themselves, they say, "Well, everyone else has lost money, too."

The Big Lie

The truth is *everyone else hasn't lost money.* Your broker hasn't. He or she makes money whether or not you do (when was the last time you got out of paying fees and commissions just because you lost some money? The mavens on Wall Street haven't. They fly around in private jets paid for by your 401(k). Members of Congress haven't. They get big donations from Wall Street to keep things going the way they are (about $2 billion a year). The corporate media haven't. They get advertising billions from those very same people.

Am I saying these people are all Madoffs and out to get you? Not at all. All I am saying is the system has been so tilted in their favor for so long that it led inexorably to the meltdown that crashed the housing market, put 8 million people out of work, and overnight wiped out 17 trillion in retirement savings and wealth…twice in 10 years. Now a lot of that is back. It might be a good time to get off this train before it is too late.

It isn't too late. Not only have the above not lost money in the meltdown; nor have the millions of people, including our clients, who have discovered the latest breed of "hybrid" annuities. This is a wonderful new concept, created by the insurance industry during the 1990s to compete with the soaring stock market. And compete it has. So much so that as mentioned previously, the SEC tried its best in 2008 (completely turning a blind eye to the abuses that did crash the markets) to regulate them out of existence, but the courts and Congress stepped in and saved them.

So exactly what are they and why are they important to you? Hybrid Annuities, aka Fixed Index Annuities (FIAs) provide you with a portion of the market upside with none of the downside.

Consider this quote by Donald Trump from "The Art of the Deal": "As long as the basic concept remained intact—no downside for me and a 50% share in the upside—it was an extraordinary deal."

This is the basis of what fixed indexed annuities do for you...they completely eliminate the downside and give you a portion of the upside of the stock market with no market risk whatsoever.

Here's how it works. The interest rate the annuity pays you is tied to a market index, such as the S&P 500. You should know that all FIAs limit what you can earn (but remember they completely eliminate market risk, as long as you abide by the contract terms). So they may have a cap, a spread, a participation rate or some other mechanism to limit their payouts. This is not done to skim profit off the top, it is a necessary component of the mechanism that makes these products possible. This is beyond the purview of this book, but we will be happy to fully explain this to you if you wish to pursue this further. In a nutshell, however, none of your money is actually in the market. Only your interest rate is tied to it; all of your principal and accrued earnings are in the insurance company's very safe general fund. Think CD safe.

Assume now that you started in an annuity when the S&P 500 was at 1000, and the annuity has a 7% cap* (this is the maximum payout for the year).

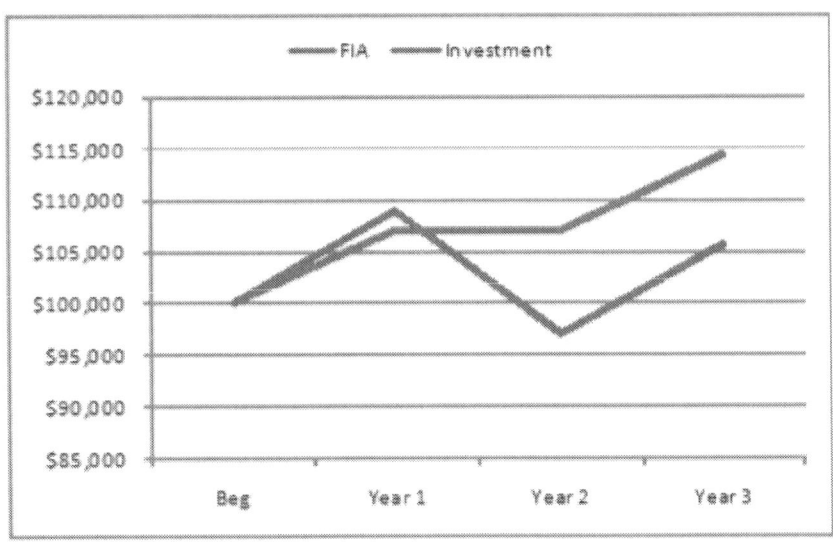

Figure 14: Simple graph showing FIA vs. S&P 500 for three year period

*****Caps have fluctuated quite a bit in the past three or four years with the prolonged period of low interest rates. However, there are many crediting options available that can maximize gains. Many of our clients are even now enjoying returns of 5%-8%.**

After year one it's the S&P 500 is at 1100 for a 10% increase. This is reflected in Figure 14. The investment starts at $100,000. The FIA goes up by 7%, the full amount provided by the cap. The investment fund (market) went up by 8.9%, the amount of the index increase less the 1.1% fee.

During the second year the market fell by 10%. Now logically, the investment fund should be showing even, but remember there are fees charged...whether you make or lose money. Plus, the 10% loss was on the full amount, not just the original $100,000. Therefore the investment fund is now in negative territory at $97,030, but the FIA is still showing $107,000 due to the annual lock-in. Now the market goes up 10% again in year three. The investment fund starts at $97,030, goes up 10% (minus 1.1% fees) and ends up at $105,762. But the annuity, because of the annual reset, starts at $107,000. So even though it only gets 70% of the upside, it got NONE of the downside and is way ahead of the market.

Now you are off and running. The investment fund will have a very difficult time ever catching up with the annuity.

But wait...what about the caps? What if the market goes up 30% and I have a cap of 7%? Well, that can happen. But that's where a good advisor that understands these policies comes into play, because there are many "crediting strategies" available. Some use caps, some use participation rates (ex. 50% of the upside), some use spreads (100% of everything after the first 5%). There are annual point to point, monthly average, monthly point to point, etc. However, the bottom line is you got into this to get away from the risk, right? And what goes along with potential upside of 30%? Right! 30%, or even more, downside!

The thing to remember is that you have lots of options to maximize your gain, and we can help you with that. But, unlike in a securities investment, you have NO RISK of losing any money. So, if we guess wrong, you might make 12% interest one year instead of 15%. But if your broker guesses wrong, you could LOSE 30% of your holdings!

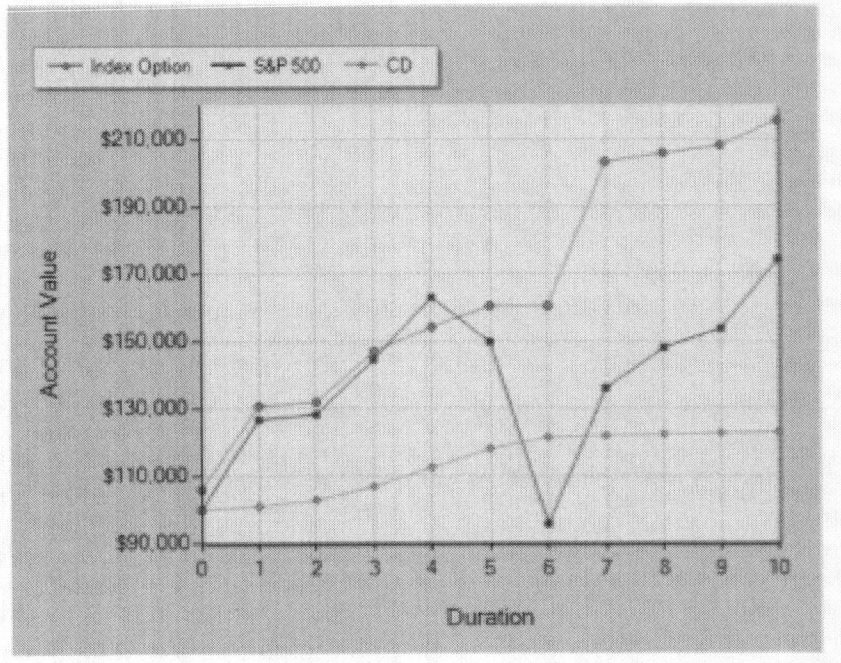

Figure 15: Sample FIA vs. CDs and S&P 500, April 15, 2003 to April 15, 2013

Above is an actual chart comparing the S&P 500, CDs and one of our favorite FIA crediting strategies during the 10 year period from April 15, 2003 to April 15, 2013. It was provided by a third-party software program that takes thousands of different cases and blends them into one statistically correct illustration.

Note how the FIA way out-performed both the market and CDs. When the market went up, so did the FIA. When it went down, all principal and profits were locked in. No market risk and great return, with all the safety and more of CDs.

This is why we like these plans. Because they provide an outcome that is nearly ideal for the client, and for us.

I say this to you with all sincerity; if you can find a better deal, go for it. But please call us and tell us about it!

"How can you know what you should do if you don't know what you can do?" — Stephen Kelley

Receive lifetime income without giving up control of your money

This is something that only insurance companies can provide, and makes planning for retirement extraordinarily easy compared to a traditional money manager.

Long life vs. Good life

As mentioned before, when you plan for income from your savings, you have to plan for one (or two) individuals. You don't know how long you will live, but you have to plan for a long life, and try to balance that against taking the maximum amount of income so you can have a good life! But the two are always in conflict. Long life says you spend less. Good life says you spend more and run the risk of running out of money. So if you believe your advisor you will spend no more than 4% of your investments every year. If you believe Morningstar and T. Rowe Price, you will spend even less. That means if you have accumulated $1 million, you get income of $40,000 per year, or less. And you thought you were going to be rich!

The insurance company doesn't have to do this. It knows exactly how long you will live, and so can give you the exactly correct amount of money to live the best and longest life possible.

Well, it doesn't really know how long you will live, but it isn't dealing with just you. It is dealing with tens, maybe hundreds of thousands of individuals with needs very similar to yours. So it can calculate with scientific certainty how many people will live to what ages. And since you are in that pool with an annuity, you get to take advantage of it.

This isn't pie in the sky. This is scientific and economic fact, and it is what has allowed the insurance industry to pocket billions and billions of dollars. In the past you had to annuitize, or give up your pool of money to take advantage of this. Now, for your parents, that wasn't such a big deal. They were used to thinking of the "defined benefits": the income stream. You, however, have been taught to look at the "defined contribution": the pot of money you have invested. When you come at it from that perspective, it's much less attractive to annuitize, even though that's the best way to maximize income.

So once again, the industry responded with brand new strategies just for you. They came up with something called the income rider, which was covered briefly in the VA section. The income rider allows you to take advantage of the insurance company's ability to provide you income based on the "law of large numbers" without giving up control of your money.

As with VAs, imagine your money is divided into two pools. One pool is your "walk away balance." This is driven by the indexing discussed in the previous passage. When the market goes up, so does your balance. When the market goes down, you are locked in, never to lose a dime. After the surrender period, you can walk away with this balance, less any withdrawals.

Now, the other pool is comprised of a source of money for lifetime income. And it grows not just based on the indexing, but also by a fixed guarantee. That guarantee is usually in the 6-8% range, so it is likely to double every 10 years. So, if you started 20 years ago with $100,000, today you would have around $400,000 for income.

Now, the insurance company uses that number to calculate your income payout. If you started at age 50, and are now age

70, your payout factor would be 6% (remember, your traditional planner can only give you 4%, and that isn't guaranteed!). So under our scenario you get $24,000 in income guaranteed for the rest of your life, no matter how long you live and no matter what the market does, all based on an initial investment of $100,000!

This is financial magic! And it's only available from annuities.

Now, assume you only collect that $24,000 for a few years, and then you die, or better yet, just change your mind. In the old model, when you had to annuitize, your money would have been gone, and you were stuck with the payouts until you died. As I mentioned, some people call it committing "annuicide."

Not anymore. Under this model, we go back to that other pool of money, the "walk away balance." That has been continuing to accumulate the entire time you have been taking withdrawals. So, you just deduct the total amount of the withdrawals from your walk away balance, and you get to…you got it…walk away with the balance!

Okay, one more thing before we move on. What if the "walk away balance" out-performs the guaranteed rollup rate on the income account? Do you get to take advantage of that?

You bet. The income account can be more, but never less than the walk away balance. So, if you have remarkable years like we have over the past several years and the annuity performs very well on the walk away side, you take advantage of that. Every year the balance is reviewed. If the income account is less than the walk away, it gets adjusted upwards to the walk away balance, and then starts accumulating at 6-8% all over again.

"(A)nd you will know the truth, and the truth will make you free."
— John 8:32

Last Things First: The key to successful income planning

Now let's put it all together. I've been doing this income planning thing now for a decade and a half, and I planned and saved for myself for many decades before that. So I have some experience with this, and I have seen things that work and things that don't. I can tell you, I like working with things that work a whole lot better.

I like sales. Do you? I like going to a store and purchasing something of value for less than it would normally cost. I almost always purchase things like this. I buy plane tickets on discount Internet sites, I buy beautiful cars used, after someone else has paid for the depreciation, I purchase my clothing at discount, food, you name it. My wife is even worse than I am. When she sees something on sale, she'll buy it whether she needs it or not! But my savings allow us to have enough, so I don't mind.

So why wouldn't I want to fund my retirement at a sale price? I would! Wouldn't you if you knew how? Well stay tuned, because you can, and I am going to show you how right now.

Think about how life works. We are on a time continuum, each day one after the other, for all the days of our lives, until they run out. The thing is, we don't know how many days that is, so as mentioned before, we have no way of knowing how much to save. This is why those commercials on TV that talk about some kind of orange magic number crack me up. How can you possibly know what your number is if you don't know how long you are going to live?

But, as mentioned earlier, the actuaries of the world have ways of figuring this stuff out. So all we have to do is employ the fruits of their labors and it makes it all much easier. The thing is, these actuarial calculations are simply tools like any others, and unless you know how to employ the tools, you won't get an optimum result.

So let's think about this time continuum. Assume that it takes $100 a day to cover your expenses. To make this easier we won't include inflation, but when we are actually planning, of course we will.

Now multiply that $100 a day by the statistical likelihood you will be alive to need it. If I am talking about tomorrow, it's very close to 100%, so I will need to have to pay my expenses the following:

$$\$100 \times 100\% = \$100$$

But what if I could pay now for days down the line? For example, what if I chose to pay for my very late in life days today? Could I get them at a discount? On sale, if you will?

Well, we know that if I am 65 I have a 50% chance of living to life expectancy of 80, and a 25% chance of living until my mid-90s. But if I am 79, I have a much better statistical chance of living to 80, right? So if I wait until then to pay for it, I won't get the sale price. This is called forward planning.

So if I were to invest today to cover the cost of my life in my 80s, I should expect to pay much less than if I waited until then.

$$\$100 \times 50\% = \$50$$

So I need to find someone who is able to give me odds, and fortunately, that's exactly what the actuaries do. They make bets on whether we will be alive or not at any given time.

When you purchase life insurance, you are making the bet you will die before you are finished financially. You give the life insurance company money, and if you die while your policy is in force, the company pays a benefit to your beneficiaries. Annuities are simply the opposite side of the same bet, except now you are betting you will live. I don't know about you, but that sounds a lot better to me.

Guaranteed Income4Life

Data Source		
● Local	Primary Age:	60
○ Master	Spouse Age:	60
○ SPIA	Year Income to Start:	20
	Rollup Rate (Rider):	6.5%
☑ Equitrust	Amount Allocated to Income:	140,000
☑ Two Lives	Bonus Amount:	10.0%
☐ Forethought	Index Rate:	5.5%
	Inflation Rate:	0.0%
	Monte Carlo Rate (assuming 90% success):	3.0%
	Market Rate:	8.0%
	Rollup Term (yrs):	20

	Gross Income		Compare	
	Single Life	Joint Life	Rider Income	WS Income
Income Rider Income:	39,338	36,312	726,242	371,944
Monte Carlo Income:	19,576	19,576	Guaranteed!	Who Knows?
Amount Needed for MC Income:	1,311,271	1,311,271	354,298 More!	

Fig. 1: Income for Life Calculator

So, what's it cost to purchase $36,000 a year income at age 80 if I am 60 today? Going to my handy-dandy income calculator, shown above, I see that if I put away $140,000, I have all my living expenses from 80 on paid for. This is a great deal. If I just assumed I would live to age 90, the cost of living doing forward planning would be $360,000. $140k is less than half!

But this leaves out a very important element of income planning. See, each block of income is calculated as lifetime income from the time income starts. Therefore, adding income to each segment has the added benefit of helping to keep up with inflation. The other thing missing here, of course is income for the years prior to age 80. So how am I going to cover those years? Simple. All these things come together in a bucketed approach to income planning.

We use different types of tools for different purposes. For example, there is one annuity that begins paying out at 8% until the contract runs out of money, and then reverts to about half that for the rest of your life, *after all of the funds are exhausted*. The only caveat is you have to leave it in the contract for 10 years before starting income. However, during that time the income base accumulates, guaranteed, at no less the 5.5%.

So adding that to the middle bucket requires $450,000 for a $360,000 a year payout at 8%. If I use Excel to calculate the present value of $450,000 it works out to:

PV(0.055,10,0,450000,1) = ($263,443)

So now, if I allocate $263,000 income for ages 70+, I will have provided $36,000 a year for years one through ten (that's usually how long it takes to deplete the value of the annuity), and then about half that for years 80 and above. This means I won't need the whole $140k for years 89+; I will only need half that if I don't care about inflation. So, the following amount takes care of income from 70 on:

$263,443 + $70,000 = $333,443

Now this is huge. If I just wanted to put savings away for enough income for that 20 year period of time, I would have to allocate $720k ($36,000 x 20). Further, this would only provide 20 years of income, whereas doing it with the income annuities ensures income no matter how long I live...85-95-105, whatever. Income is mine for the duration. And not just me. It covers both my lifespan and my wife's!

What would it cost to do this using forward planning in the market? Well, still using the same assumptions of age 60 now with income beginning in 10 years at age 70, if I use the 4% rule, I would need to grow my $333,443 to $900,000 by age 70. That would require a 10.44% rate of return, every year, net of taxes and fees. How likely is that? But the annuity is a 100% certainty. No guessing, no ifs, ands or buts.

Now, add to that number my Social Security benefits if I work until age 70, along with any pensions I have, as well as those my wife has, and I have a pretty healthy retirement. Guaranteed.

This is only one scenario, and isn't meant to imply that all cases should be handled in this way. It's just an example. But the fundamentals used here, even if different strategies and products need to be employed, are universal. Use safe, guaranteed products that derive their value from actuarial calculations, and fit them in where they belong. It's what every pension plan, state lottery, and annuity contract has been doing forever.

This really isn't rocket science. It's just using the right tools and a little common sense.

Lessons from the street

"So I feel like he's telling me that in order to retire, I have to be rich or be a gambler," she said, her voice taking on a tone of resignation and desperation. "But I don't have a choice. I'm worn out and just can't continue to work and take care of my husband anymore." She was almost in tears. "Something has to give. Please just tell me what you think I should do."

This meeting had started off okay, but I could sense her unease. She was a very nice woman in her early 60s who carried herself in a way that bespoke determination in the face of desperation. I had learned she was a nurse of many years who had taken an early retirement in 2006 so she and her older husband could have some quality time together. They'd had a nice nest egg, and it had all started well with a family trip to France. Then the crash happened and they had lost a substantial amount. This was made worse by the fact that they were also trying to live on their now depleted investments, and they felt they were just depleting it even faster. When they couldn't take it anymore they had sold off all their stocks and bonds and moved their money into CDs, and tried living on what was left along with his Social Security.

They were just barely getting by when he'd gotten sick, and in a desperation move she'd gone back to work. Now he was failing rapidly mentally but was still physically strong, and she was finding that trying to be the primary caretaker and breadwinner wasn't working. As his dementia deepened, she felt the man she loved slipping away and she was wrestling with whether she should commit him to a home, or alternatively to retire and be a full-time caregiver, which was clearly what she'd prefer.

If she put him in a home, his Social Security income would be allocated to his care and she would be in a real pinch financially, especially since what retirement assets they had were in his name, and she was fearful that would be depleted completely. If she stayed home, she could begin to take her own benefit, but that would not come close to filling the gap created by her loss of employment. She would receive a small pension, but not much, and all that was left was her $400,000 IRA. To top it all off, she was full of guilt about having decided against opting for a long term care plan when they had been able to do so. But their financial position had seemed so strong at the time and people she trusted had counselled against it, saying it was just a waste of money.

She figured if she could get $20,000-$22,000 from her IRA, she could just squeak by. Her current advisor had explained that at her age she had the potential to live another 30 years or longer, and his advice had been to put it back in the market so she could get some rate of return, as she was clearly not going to be able to get a sustainable interest rate that would provide enough for that period of time. He felt a 60/40 mix of equities and bonds would be appropriate, and perhaps a variable annuity as well. He felt if she was aggressive in her mix she could get enough return to make ends meet by taking a 5% annual withdrawal. When we spoke she said she felt he made sense, but she was still gun shy about the market and had heard a lot of negative things about annuities and was looking for a second opinion. Her sister, who is a client of mine, had told her about me. After listening to our radio show for a few weeks she decided to give me a try.

Clearly mistakes had been made. She should have never passed up the opportunity to do some kind of planning for a potential long-term care event; we each have a 70% chance of needing some kind of care in our lifetime. The mistake is a common one. People hate to buy insurance and there is a general "it'll never happen to me" attitude out there. However, her advisor should have shown her some of the non-LTC insurance alternatives. When you have means, as they clearly had at one point, there are numerous things that can be done to protect those means, but it does take some careful thought and planning. I tend to press this issue with clients, even though it sometimes makes me seem like a nagging insurance guy out for another commission. I can assure you it is not that at all. Stories like these break my heart and whenever I can do something to protect a client, it fills me with a great sense of purpose and gratitude.

The second thing that should never have been allowed was for all of their assets to remain at risk in the market once they retired. It is imperative to move money allocated for income into an asset class that will protect your money from market risk as well as provide guaranteed lifetime income. Anything short of that simply does not do the job. When you build your house on sand, it doesn't matter how impressive and big and strong it appears to be, the sand underneath will inevitably give away. Risk-based assets are called that for a reason. Risk is okay to an extent when building wealth, but it has no place at all in an income plan. Where is the line item in your plan that calls for losing 40-50% of your income-producing assets? Exactly. So why haven't you done anything about it?

However none of this was what she needed to hear from me, so I didn't get into it. She was desperate for help and was getting ready to repeat her mistakes with a menu of very risky assets that would not address her underlying problems. So I took a very careful look at her situation and, in the end, recommended an immediate lifetime annuity for $300,000. I considered it a pretty radical move. I normally don't use immediate annuities; they require you to give up control of your money, and the income stream dies when you do. But in her case she had very few options, her back was against the wall, and she needed maximum guaranteed income that would last her lifetime and that's the tool to use when you need it. At her age she qualified for a 6.18% lifetime income which worked out to about $18,500 a year; very close to her bottom line need. Further, by using a Medicaid-friendly immediate annuity, I was able to provide this income for her to live out her life knowing it would never be consumed by Medicaid if and when he needed the care, which looked inevitable.

In addition, that left her $100,000 which we put into the bank. This money is for emergencies, is below the Medicaid threshold, and would provide her emergency funds should she need them. It's not a perfect plan, but none are. And at least now she is sleeping at night and feeling like she has some options.

"Rule #1: Never lose the money. Rule #2: See rule number one."
—Warren Buffett

How Safe is "Safe"?

Fixed annuities and life insurance contracts emphasize safety above everything else. In fact, financial experts consider fixed annuities and life insurance, CDs and treasuries as the safest monetary instruments available. And of the three, fixed life insurance products have by far the very best track record.

Now I know how that sounds. Please just read on and I will explain why that is.

People often wonder if annuities are FDIC insured. And the answer is no, they are not. But they actually have a better record of depositor protection in the event of company failure than the FDIC.

How can this be?

Fixed insurance and annuity policies are protected by the Legal Reserve System. The Legal Reserve System dictates and enforces very strict controls and safety measures on how money under its oversight is managed.

Why is FDIC Insurance necessary?

Banks can have up to a nine-to-one ratio of liabilities to capital. Here's what that means. If you deposit $1,000 in a bank, the bank can go to the Federal Reserve and borrow up to $9,000 against that $1,000. Then, the bank can lend that money out to personal loans, credit cards, run businesses, and all of the other commercial lending activities a bank engages in.

They get in trouble, however, when they start to get greedy like what happened during the years prior to 2008 when they started lending to financial markets and investing in derivatives and all kinds of things commercial banks were never supposed to do. Before we knew it, they were swimming in mountains of debt they couldn't pay back and the whole system came down.

Obviously, banks can easily become over-leveraged, and sometimes in very risky investments, like those that led to the recent financial and banking crisis of 2008, and the Great Depression of the 1930s. FDIC insurance is critical for safety and protecting depositors from a financial meltdown like happened in the 30s. However, as we saw in 2008, even these measures were not enough to prevent another catastrophe.

Why the Legal Reserve System is Different

First, Legal Reserve life insurance companies are legally prohibited from speculating with your money. Unlike banks, markets or any other financial system, 100% of their investment of your money must, by law, be invested in the very safest monetary vehicles available.

Most goes into long-term investment-grade bonds, treasuries, and extremely conservative real estate and other types of commercial developments.

Second, life insurance companies are required by law to maintain a greater than one-to-one ratio of their capital to their liabilities. If they bring in a dollar, unlike banks, they cannot lend nine, or six, or three, or even one dollar. They can lend out (invest) only what is left over after the reserve fund is set aside.

A large percentage of each premium dollar calculated by actuaries for each company goes into the policy owner's reserve fund. This policy reserve (Legal Reserve) fund is a liability to the life insurance company. The fund is established as a way of determining or measuring the assets the company must maintain in order to be able to meet its future commitments under the policies it has issued. In other words, the reserve liabilities are established as financial safeguards to ensure the company will have sufficient assets to pay its claims and other commitments when they fall due. These assets are kept intact for payment of living and death benefits to the insured. In other words, the insurance company isn't backing your money, your money is!

If an insurance company's reserve levels fall short and it is unable to correct the situation, it goes into what is called receivership. The remaining insurance companies in the state legal reserve pool must assume the liabilities and obligations of the insurer. The reserve pool protects fixed annuity investors as well as those who purchase other life insurance products or policies.

Third, Legal Reserve Life Insurers are members of reinsurance groups. If you purchase an annuity from Company A, Company A has secured agreements from Companies B, C, and D to help cover its liabilities. Each company has from four to a dozen other companies backing its contracts.

Fourth, insurance companies don't have to comply just with one governing body like banks, they must satisfy the safety requirements of all 50 states. Every year all legal reserve life insurance companies submit annual statements to the insurance departments of each state in which they are licensed to do business. These are detailed reports of an insurance company's financial status that is important in evaluating the company's solvency and compliance with the insurance laws. Companies found not to comply with their reserve requirements have their operations suspended immediately and are prohibited from selling more policies until they have taken corrective action.

In the unlikely event that a company's annual statement or its own examination reveals possible financial weakness, one of several avenues is open to the company:

- Produce additional operating capital;
- Sell its business to another life company;
- Merge into another financially stable life company.

A legal reserve life insurance company does not simply close its doors and go out of business declaring that all policies are null and void. Legal reserve life policyholders enjoy personal security safeguards unknown by other type of financial industry.

Fifth, if one company is purchased or merged into another, there is no change whatsoever in the policy benefits or premiums. Your contract would be just as binding on the new company as it was on the company you originally purchased it from.

So, the bottom line is in order to lose any money in a fixed life insurance or annuity policy due to company insolvency, ALL of the following would have to happen.

- Your insurance company's very safe bond portfolio would have to fail.
- Your surplus fund would have to be depleted.
- The very safe bond portfolios of all four to 14 reinsurance partners would have to fail, along with their reserve funds.
- The state reserve fund would have to fail.
- There would have to be no company left that could merge with the failing company, i.e., a complete financial meltdown far worse than anything we have ever seen before.

This confluence of events has never happened in the history of the Legal Reserve System.

I promised proof at the beginning of this section that the Legal Reserve System had a better track record than the FDIC.

Legal Reserve companies had their strongest showing of strength during the Great Depression of 1929-1938 when some 9,000 banks suspended operations while 99% of all fixed life insurance in force continued unaffected.

Many people are not aware that it was not the government that bailed out the banking industry during the Great Depression; it was the U.S. insurance industry. Without it, we would never have pulled out of the Great Depression with our financial system intact. People often question this statement as it is not well publicized. Here are the facts. According to the U.S. Department of Commerce, during the time of the Great Depression the insurance industry pumped over $18 billion into the nation's economy. If you adjust the dollars based on percentage of GDP, using the average GDP of the 10 years of the Great Depression, that equates to around three to six trillion in today's dollars! At the same time its assets and ability to pay actually increased from:

> 1929..................................$18,010,000,000
>
> 1934..................................$23,334,308,702
>
> Representing a gain of $5,324,308,702

The FDIC is a government agency tasked with insuring depositors against the over-leveraging that is at the core operating principle of the American banking system, and which caused the crash of the thirties and later the 2000s. During the 30s the insurance industry rescued the United

States economy. During the crash of 2008 when hundreds of banks failed (in spite of FDIC insurance) most insurance carriers had their ratings reaffirmed by the ratings agencies. And once again, not one person in a fixed annuity or life policy lost a dime in the melt down.

Even AIG, which was at the heart of much of the problem with its plan to corner the market on credit default swaps, had its life and annuity division's (American General Life) ratings reaffirmed. In fact they wanted to raid the $400 billion in capitalization they had in reserve to rescue the parent company, but the state insurance departments and federal government would not allow it, since the money belonged not to AIG, but to the policy holders who had taken out the insurance.

The truth is, the United States insurance system is the most secure financial system on earth with over one trillion dollars in reserve capitalization. It is far more solvent than the U.S. Government and U.S. banking system combined. FDIC insurance was created in response to the bank failures of the 1930s. It did not include the insurance industry because there was no need; it already had the proven safeguards of the Legal Reserve System in place.

Had the banking industry complied by these same safeguards, there may never have been a Great Depression, and we would certainly not have gone through the problems of 2008.

You don't have to take our word for it. Even Ben Bernanke, former Chairman of the Federal Reserve and the man in charge of the United States government's monetary policy, understands how safe these policies are. He has most of his retirement plan invested in annuities. If anyone should understand what is safe and what isn't he should!

Variations on a theme

"But, is it safe?" This is one of the most perplexing questions I get from people who are considering using our income planning services. More often than not, they are referring to an annuity or other life insurance product we sell, and are really struggling with how safe they are. I know this is a genuine concern…I just know it. But, I also know it's entirely irrational.

"What…irrational?" you say. Yep, that's exactly what I said, and here's why. Most of the people doubting the safety of these products are people who have much, if not most, of their retirement savings in…you guessed it…the stock market! In addition, most of these people have at one time or another lost a great deal of their savings in the market, and if pressed, will tell you they expect it to happen again. And yet they are very reluctant to get out for fear of missing the NEXT BIG BULL MARKET.

I have news for you. This is the next big bull market, and what happens after all bull markets? A bear market, right? So here we are, sitting on a pile of winnings from this BIG BULL MARKET, and instead of taking their winnings off the table, these people do what gamblers always do…they are doubling down.

"But it always comes back," a prospect told me the other day. "If it goes down again, I'll just ride it out like I did the last time." Yeah, this makes a lot of sense, doesn't it? Last time this guy was still ten years away from retirement. This time, if it happens again, he will have to delay his retirement for another ten years, or even longer. I know this, because he told me so when I asked what would happen if we went through another 2008. His response was he'd just wait it out, because it always bounces right back, right?

Now this is just crazy talk. Let's say you are 67 years old and getting ready to hang it up. You have $700k saved up and are feeling pretty good about things. The next thing you know, your $700k is $400k, and instead of getting $28,000 a year out of it, you are going to get only $16,000 a year in income, and if you believe Morningstar, you are going to run a 50% risk of running out of money ("Low Bond Yields and Safe Portfolio Withdrawal Rates," 2013, Morningstar).

And you could have completely avoided this "safe" scenario if you had gone with a "risky" income annuity. Here's why. First, if you use a fixed, or fixed index annuity, you can never lose any money. Each year interest is credited to your account and then locked in, becoming the base for future interest calculations. It's just like a CD or a savings account, only much safer and on steroids.

Secondly, and even more importantly, you spread the risk of outliving your money. You do this by putting yourself in a large pool of lives. The insurance company can calculate with near exact precision how long the average life span of the pool will be. The money, which is locked into the pool and stabilized by surrender charges (these really do work in your favor, in spite of the noise and propaganda from Wall Street), will earn a predictable rate of return. At this point it's a simple calculation: (Initial deposit x predictable rate of return)/life expectancy.

The insurance company can therefore guarantee a lifetime payout. That payout is often two to three times the payout you can safely take out of your investment accounts. In the $700k example above, the retiree could only take $28,000 with a 50% chance of running out of money, but with a split annuity strategy, that same person could have received nearly $50,000, guaranteed for the rest of his or her life.

Often people will call the strength of the guarantee into question (back to the top of this column). They are often put off by the disclaimer: "Annuity guarantees are backed by the claims paying ability of the issuing carrier." Let's put this one to bed right now. In the history of these products, we cannot point to a single individual who has lost money in a fixed life or annuity contract, as long as they have met the terms of the contract. It's the most stable and secure financial industry in the world. It has to be. Insurance is designed to protect your assets. Markets are designed to speculate with them.

We take a lot of abuse from our fellow financial professionals over our preference for annuities when it comes to income planning. We get accused of just being greedy, commission-based salespeople (that's rich, coming from Wall Street, don't you think?) who don't care about our clients. But what if we aren't? What if we do this because we know they are the right thing for the job?

Look at it this way. Assume for the sake of argument you have one store that sells dishwashers and one that sells clothes washers. Now the dishwasher salesman wants to corner the market for all the washers, so he goes on a campaign to discredit the clothes washer salesman. He points to the fact that if you put your dishes in the clothes washer, they are going to break (duh!). He whips up a frenzy about those knives and forks whipping around. These things are just plain dangerous! Not only that, if you wash your clothes in them they can shrink and more often than not, come out wrinkled. Worst of all, think of all that money that greedy clothes washer salesman is going to make on commissions, especially when he tries to sell you a dryer, too!

But the thing that's never, ever discussed is the fact that you simply cannot effectively wash clothes in a dishwasher! Nor can you safely take income from a risk-based asset. It all sounds pretty absurd, doesn't it? As absurd as gambling with your retirement funds? You tell me.

"The difference between stupidity and genius is that genius has its limits." — Albert Einstein

The 10 Most Common Objections to Annuities

10. "I don't want to tie up my money."

I get it. Where is the most liquid place you can think of to put your money? Money market accounts? Checking? Savings? Your mattress? Why don't you put of all your money in these locations? Because you need a return that will grow your money and fight inflation. You may also need an income that these low or no-yield accounts can't give.

"By the way, where is your money now?" I often ask. If your answer is "in the market," then you're violating your own liquidity principle. Bear with me. I realize you can sell anytime you want…

But if you called your broker during a down market, how much of what you gave him could he send you? 50%? 60%? Less? On $100,000 let's say he sent you $50,000 (which is all that's left due to the market's volatility). You call him up to tell him you received the $50,000 and ask how long it will be before you get the other $50,000. He informs you that if you want the second $50,000 you have to return the first $50,000 and then wait a long time… and maybe you will get it back. In other words, you may have little or no liquidity.

With an FIA the worst your liquidity could be damaged would be to return all but about 10%-12% (again – worst case – usually much lower) due to surrender charges. However, you have the opportunity to take 10% annually with no penalty, adding up to withdrawing your entire original premium in 10 years (or a little longer, depending on your return, and whether the 10% is calculated on the original premium every year or the new account value). Do you have a plan in place to spend your entire principal in ten years?

So, with an annuity you know up front what the worst case scenario will be. And because you know the facts without a doubt, you can do actual planning. (Remember the title of this booklet.)

9. "I don't get all the up – caps and participation rates are limiting."

It's true that you don't get all the up with an FIA. However, it is not a disadvantage to get some of the up and none of the down compared to what most people get. Actually, with your diversified portfolio, not only are you not getting all the up, but you are participating in some of the down. Personally, I would rather get some of the up and none of the down than to get some of the up and some of the down. (Some of my clients got over 20% in the last year. How did you do?)

Warren Buffett thinks diversified portfolios reduce your return. If you had put all your money in just the winner in your portfolio you would have made more, but because we can't know that in advance we diversify, allowing the losers to offset the winners, resulting in an averaged return, which is less than the broad market's performance in most years as represented by the S&P 500. So when you diversify you aren't getting all of the up, but you are participating in the down, unlike in the fixed index annuity.

8. "I don't like surrender charges."

Surrender charges are voluntary and self-imposed if more than a 10% penalty-free withdrawal is made in a given year. Let's say you had a charge as high as 12% (worst case) for an amount taken above the 10% penalty-free withdrawal. Let's use the example of a $20,000 withdrawal from a $100,000 account. The first $10,000 is penalty free. The second 10,000 withdrawal would incur a 12% charge ($1,200). $1,200 is 1.2% of your $100,000 account. Let's also assume that you made 8% on your account's growth in the same year. Effectively, what you have done is to withdraw 20% of the account and reduced your 8% interest to 6.8% as a result of the fee. I tell people in the rare cases when they need more than 10% to go ahead and take it. It's not the end of the world.

I understand printed surrender charges, which are disclosed before you buy an annuity, seem scary. "What if I need my money and I have to pay a fee to get it?" is likely what you are thinking. But…have you ever signed a prospectus that basically said you can lose your shirt, but because there is not a printed schedule of the market's volatility charges and because you think everybody else is doing it, it must be okay?

I have had people come into my office and show me statements with as much as 50% losses; but because it was not in print in the form of a penalty schedule before they bought, they bought anyway. I have never seen an annuity with a 50% surrender charge. Surrender charges are in your control and don't come into play unless you make that choice. Further, the market's volatility charges happen to you involuntarily. One more thing…there is such a thing as a Fixed Indexed Annuity that delivers 100% liquidity of the initial premium any time you want it, with no surrender charges!

7. "My broker doesn't like index annuities."

No kidding. Over the last 10 years, more than $2.3 trillion of annuity products have been sold in the United States. The overwhelming majority of those sales were into deferred annuity products with the primary intention of tax-deferred growth. Guess where that money came from. In addition, the amount of money the industry can charge in fees on has shrunk dramatically in the past few years, due to the market meltdown. Not only doesn't your broker like them, the whole investment community doesn't like them.

It shouldn't surprise you that your broker or anyone else doesn't like anything he views as having the possibility of taking your accounts away from him or her. It's like ripping the braces off his kid's teeth (or that's the way he/she may see it!) I have not met many brokers who don't sell FIAs who actually understand them themselves, much less have the ability to be able to fairly and accurately explain them to their clients. In any event, who are you trying to please? Yourself or your broker? By the way, ask your broker if fixed annuities are bad, why are variable annuities good? Could it have something to do with all the fees they get to charge?

6. "My broker told me your commissions are too high."

I don't mind telling you that the longest, highest paying FIA I sell has a commission of about 2/3-1% per year. More often than not, the broker who is telling you not to buy because of high commissions is in all likelihood being paid as much as 2% per year, or three times what I get paid. And, if he is selling variable annuities (show me one who isn't), you are probably being charged around 4% per year...six times what an index annuity costs.

Further, the broker's compensation and VA fees come out of your funds. That means whether you make money or lose money, YOU will pay your broker that fee! How did you do last year? Did you lose money? Did you pay your broker for the privilege?

And these fees are expensive! If you make 6% on your money and your broker takes 2-4%, he's getting one to two thirds of your total profits...and you take all the risk!

With a Fixed Index Annuity, my commission is paid directly by the insurance company. Not a penny comes out of your funds as long as you abide by the terms of the contract. 100%

of your money is working and growing for you. The only time you would ever be charged is if you take your money out early, over the 10%annual free withdrawals, in which case the insurance company asks that you help cover the charges caused by the early withdrawal (surrender charges).

Even better. If you are willing to give away a small part of the upside, you can get into an annuity that will return 100% of your initial deposit to you any time you want, with only interest penalties.

5. "The index calculations don't include dividends."

It's true. Again, you won't get all the up. However, can you give me an example of something that includes or pays dividends that has no risk to your principal or previously earned gains? It's not a perfect world, and I admit I'm not offering perfection; but I remind you again that you already own an imperfect investment…and one where you could lose your shirt (not possible with an FIA!).

4. "My broker says FIAs aren't appropriate for qualified funds such as IRAs and 401(k)s."

Since when is tax treatment the only consideration given concerning whether anyone should buy a product or make an investment? It's true that from a tax standpoint it's a wash; but what about safety, opportunity and liquidity? All of these should be considered as well. When looking at the complete picture most people agree that it makes sense to have some money in an FIA. This product is not likely to duplicate any other investment you have. We are all taught to diversify, and an FIA is a great way to do it. Think about safely linking to the horsepower of 500 stocks represented in the S&P 500 as compared to owning a couple of stocks directly. This is much greater diversification.

3. "Can I trust an insurance company with my money?"

I find it interesting that people trust insurance companies with insuring their homes, cars, health and life, but not their nest eggs and future income. If we can feel okay about trusting them with all of this, then we ought to be okay with having them insure our nest eggs and income.

No owner of an FIA has ever suffered any losses due to a company failure, even during times when many banks and brokerage firms have failed. Even in the Great Depression, when they couldn't get their money anywhere else, people were able to redeem the cash values of their life insurance. It is the safest place I know to grow your money.

2. "I don't believe there is enough horsepower in an FIA, and I can make more in mutual funds."

We already know that the best way to grow money is to never have to make up for a loss, even for one year. Adding interest every year that has been generated from stock market indices, or a bond index or the fixed account to the highest amount you have ever had, minus your voluntary withdrawals will compete very favorably over time with a volatile market that continuously takes back previously-earned gains.

Some people call the last ten years the "Lost Decade" because many put up the capital, took the risk and have nothing to show for it. Not annuity owners! If you had been in an FIA for the same period of time, the story would have been much different and vastly better. In fact, we have some clients that doubled, or even tripled their money over that 10 year period. Did you?

Think of the market as a powerful jet plane flying at 500 mph into a 600 mph head wind. Yes it's powerful, but how far are you really going to go? Now, think of the annuity as a 300 mph nonstop bullet train with no head wind to fight. Which is going to get you there faster?

1. "The fees are too high."

That's true, if we are discussing variable annuities, which most brokers deal in. As mentioned before, these can run as high as 4% annually. However, with fixed annuities there are no fees unless an extra benefit is added on. The insurance company earns a spread between the gross of the bond portfolio's yield, which they manage, and the net is credited to your account. This spread is similar to how banks make money and typically ranges around 2% annually. From this spread the insurance company pays the agent, covers the insurance company's expenses and returns a profit to its shareholders.

The difference is that a spread is not taken from your existing account balance. So in a year where the annuity credits zero growth due to a flat or declining market, the FIA owner gets a true zero - not zero minus 2-3% in management fees, which is what happens on brokerage accounts and variable annuities (or even a loss minus 2-3%!), adding insult to injury!

Index

10% annual free withdrawals, *144*
151-a, *85*
2.8% Rule, *57, 90, 91*
2008, *46, 48, 49, 60, 69, 85, 102*
20-year term life policy, *79*
30 year planning horizon, *89*
4% rule, *118*
4% Rule, *53, 57*
401(k), 2, *6, 23, 24, 26, 27, 28, 29, 84, 97, 101*
401(k)s., *28, 144*
403(b), *29*
50/50 mix of stocks and bonds, *50*
90% success rate, *15, 53, 56, 95, 96*
ABC Financial Planning course, 9
accounting, 3
actuarial calculations, *114, 118*
actuaries, *114, 115*
advertising, *16, 101*
advice, 2, 3, *6, 13, 14, 17*
AIG, 132
America's retirement, 30
American banking system, 131
American Dream, 23, 25, 26, 28
American Express Company, *24*

American General Life, 132
American retirement system, 30
  dismantling and raiding of, 30
annua, *24*
annual point to point, *105*
annual reset, *105*
annuicide, *96, 111*
annuities, *5, 74, 75, 77, 81, 82, 83, 85, 86, 87, 92, 93, 96, 98, 102, 103, 111, 118*
annuitization, *98*
annuitize, *109, 111*
annuity, 74, 77, 78, 80, 83, 84, 86, 87, 95, 98, 103, 105, 109, 112, 117, 118, 119, 126, 128, 130, 132, 139, 140, 141, 143, 144, 146, 147
assets to pay its claims, 128
average rate of return, *55, 65*
Baby Boomer, *30*
Banks, 26, 126
bazillion, gazillion, 9
bear market, *87*
beneficiary, *77*
Bengen, William, *50*
Bernanke, Ben, 133
bond bubble, *46*
Bond prices, *71*

Bonds, *55, 61, 69*
bonus money, *27*
Boomer, *31, 45*
broker, *14, 15, 74, 101, 106, 139, 142, 143, 144*
brokerage accounts, *147*
broker-dealer, *14*
broker-dealers, *15*
brokers, *96, 142, 147*
bubble, *70*
bucket, *117*
Buffett, *46*
Buffett, Warren, *140*
Bush administration, 30
cap, *103, 104, 105*
capital, *30, 31, 48*
caps, *105, 140*
casino, 30
CDs, *106, 107,* 125
CFPB, *52*
CODA, *26*
cognitive ability and financial literacy, 7
COLA, *54, 58*
commercial banking, *26*
commercial banks, *26*
commissions, *17, 75, 99, 101, 143*
companies are legally prohibited from speculating with your money, 127
complacency, *47, 48, 49*
compliance, *15*
Conable, Barber, *27, 28*

Confidence in financial decision making abilities, 7
Congress, *25, 26, 27, 28, 86, 101, 102*
conventional wisdom, *35, 38*
corporate profits, 30
Crash, *26, 44, 54*
Crash of 1929, *26*
crash of 2008, 132
Crash of 2008, *44*
crediting strategies, *105, 106*
Cypress, *89*
Dalbar, *60, 61*
death benefit, *77, 79*
debenture bond,, *70*
deferred, *26, 35, 37, 81*
Deferred compensation arrangements, 26
deferring taxes, *38*
defined benefits, *96, 109*
defined benefits plan, *96*
Defined contribution plans, *29*
defined-contribution plans, 10
Department of Labor, *28*
depositors, *26, 51*
Depression, *25, 26*
derivatives, *46*
distressed shares, *67*
diversified portfolio, *69, 140*
diversify, *140, 145*
dividends, **144**

dollar cost averaging, *57*
dot-com, 30
Dow, *65*, *100*
Dow Jones, *100*
eliminating taxes, *35*
emotions, *47*, *60*
Employee Retirement Income Security Act of 1974, *27*
energy partnerships, *15*, *16*, *17*
equities, *29*, *70*
equity portfolio, *56*
ERISA, *27*
failure rate, *54*
FDIC, 125, 126, 130, 131, 132
FDIC insurance, 132
Federal Reserve, 45, 72, 73, 126, 133
fee, *75*, *99*, *104*, *141*, *143*
fees, *55*, *74*, *75*, *76*, *82*, *84*, *89*, *95*, *99*, *100*, *101*, *104*, *118*, *142*, *143*, *147*
FIA, *85*, *98*, *104*, *105*, *106*, *107*, *139*, *140*, *143*, *144*, *145*, *146*, *147*
FIAs, *85*, *102*, *103*, *142*, *144*
Fiduciaries
    fiduciary, fiduciaries, 12
fiduciary, *12*, *13*, *14*, *15*, *16*
financial, 3, 7
Financial Advisors, *13*
financial literacy, *7*
Financial Literacy, 7, 8

financial meltdown, 126, 130
financial planner, 4, *15*
financial safeguards, 128
financial services, *15*, *16*, *48*
Finra, *52*
fixed annuities, *86*, *142*, *147*
fixed income component, *69*
Fixed Index Annuities, *102*
Fixed Index Annuity, *98*, *99*, *143*
forward planning, *115*, *116*, *118*
free withdrawals, *144*
fund investor, *62*
funds, *29*, *30*, *57*, *61*, *75*, *77*, *81*, *117*
GDP, *46*
general fund, *93*
Glass-Steagall, *25*, *26*
    repeal under Gramm–Leach–Bliley Act, 26
government rate, *44*
government regulating body, *52*
government securities, *44*
Gramm–Leach–Bliley Act., 26
Great Depression, *25*, 126, 130, 131, 133, *145*
growth rate, *36*
guarantee income, *80*
guaranteed death benefit rider, *77*

guaranteed income, *84*
guaranteed lifetime income streams, *98*
guaranteed withdrawal income rider GWIR, GWIB, GIWB, *77*
guarantees, *74, 77, 78, 84, 86, 94*
gurufocus.com, *45*
hold it to maturity,, *71*
how long you are going to live, 11, 89, 114
Hybrid Annuities, *102*
hybrid annuity, *98*
hybrid fixed annuity, *83*
IAR, *12, 13*
immediate annuities, *96*
income amount, *81*
income base, *80, 117*
income planning success, *58*
income rider, *79, 110*
increasing gains., *65*
index annuities, *85, 86, 87*
index annuity sales abuses, *87*
index fund, *62*
inflation, 10, 32, 50, 53, 55, 114, 116, 117, 138
insurance, 5, 17, 26, 52, 75, 76, 77, 78, 79, 83, 85, 87, 88, 92, 93, 96, 102, 108, 109, 110, 115, 125, 126, 127, 128, 129, 130, 131, 132, 143, 145, 147

insurance company, *76, 79, 83, 93, 109, 110, 115, 143, 145, 147*
insurance departments of each state, 129
interest rates, *44, 45, 71, 72, 73, 104*
investment, *13, 14, 25, 44, 75, 81, 82, 84, 85, 104, 105, 111*
Investment Advisor Representative, *12, 13*
investment advisors, *13*
investment banking, 25
investment fund, *104, 105*
investment-grade bonds, 127
investor behavior, *48*
investors, *30, 44, 48, 60, 61, 62, 85*
IRA, *2, 29, 35, 36, 84*
IRAs, *35, 144*
IRS, *26*
Jane Bryant Quinn, *81*
John Biggs, *81*
Kodak, *27, 28*
Last Things First, *113*
law of large numbers, *110*
Law of Large Numbers, *88*
laws of physics, *51*
legal, 3
Legal Reserve System, 126, 127, 130, 132
legal responsibility, *16*
life expectancy, *90, 91, 92, 115*
life insurance, 2

life span, *52, 92*
lifespan, 10, *118*
lifespans, 5
lifetime payouts, *24, 98*
liquid, *138*
liquidity, *99, 138, 139, 142, 144*
long life, *91, 108*
Long life vs. Good life, *108*
long-term healthcare, 10
Lost Decade, *100, 146*
low interest rates, 10
Madoff, *101*
Madoff, Bernie, *85*
Manhattan Project, *51*
market, 21, 30, 31, 32, 33, 41, 42, 44, 45, 46, 47, 54, 55, 56, 58, 59, 60, 61, 64, 71, 75, 77, 78, 82, 84, 85, 89, 94, 96, 99, 100, 102, 103, 104, 105, 107, 110, 111, 118, 121, 122, 132, 133, 134, 136, 138, 139, 140, 141, 142, 146, 147
market bottom, *54*
Market Cap, *46*
market index, *103*
market meltdown, *142*
market participation without the risk, *99*
Market risk, 10
Marrion, Jack, *86, 87*
maximum amount of income, *108*
meltdown, *69, 102*

meltdown of 2008, *69*
Merrill Lynch, *86*
middle class, *28*
minimum guaranteed return, *80*
minimum income withdrawal benefit, *79*
Monte Carlo, *50, 52, 53, 91*
Monte Carlo planning, *51, 52*
Monte Carlo simulation, *53*
monthly average, *105*
monthly point to point, *105*
Morningstar, *56, 75, 90, 91, 95, 109*
mortality, *24, 52*
mutual funds, *146*
no fees or risk, *84*
nuclear particles, *51*
nuclear physics, *51*
oil shale partnership, *84*
outcome, 2
over-leveraged, 126
participation rates, *105, 140*
PE ratios, 42, 59
penalties, *99*
pension, *24, 81, 84, 92, 96, 119*
pension plans, *24, 92*
pensions, 10, *24, 28, 30, 118*
personal pension plan, *84*

plan, 2
plan for life expectancy, *92*
planner, *8, 50, 52, 57, 89, 90, 91, 95, 111*
policy holders, 5, 132
policy owner's reserve fund, 127
policy reserve, 127
pool of money, *97, 109, 111*
pool of people, *88, 89*
population groups, *88*
premium, *77, 79*
privatization of Social Security, 30
prospectus, *141*
protect investors from **UPSIDE RISK**, 85
provisional income, 37
prudent, *88, 89, 90, 91*
random, *51*
rate of return, *17, 55, 65, 66, 67, 80, 90, 91, 92, 95, 118*
rates of return, *44, 58, 64, 67*
Rates of return, *64*
rational thought, *47*
reduce risk, 59
Reduce taxes, *84*
Registered Investment Advisor, *13, 14*
Registered Representatives, *13*
regulators, *87*
reinsurance groups, 128
Removing risk, *65*

reserve, 5, 127, 128, 129, 130, 132
reserve funds, 130
reserve liabilities, 128
reserve to age 120, 5
retire, *24, 31, 36, 58, 93*
retirement, 4, *5, 6, 7, 8, 14, 15, 23, 25, 27, 28, 30, 31, 35, 36, 37, 38, 45, 50, 52, 56, 58, 61, 69, 70, 88, 90, 93, 98, 102, 108, 114, 118*
retirement income, 4
retirement plan income, *37*
retirement years, *38*
Revenue Act of 1978, *26*
reverse dollar cost averaging, *57*
Reverse Dollar Cost Averaging, *57, 67*
RIA, *13, 14*
rider, *77, 78, 79, 80, 93, 110*
riders, *77, 80*
risk, *16, 44, 53, 61, 66, 67, 75, 82, 83, 84, 85, 88, 89, 92, 95, 97, 99, 103, 107, 108*
risk class, 59
RMD, *84*
Roth, *2, 36*
Roth IRA, 2
Rule 151A, *87*
S&P 500, *47, 55, 62, 103, 104, 140, 145*
S&P500, *100, 106*
Safe, 56, 125

safe-money hybrid annuities, *85*
safest monetary instruments available, 125
safety, 69, 99, 107, 125, 126, 128, 144
Savage, Caroll, *27*
SEC, *52*, *85*, *86*, *88*, *89*, *102*
SEC Ruling 151-a, 85
secular markets
    secular bull and bear markets, 42
secure income, *16*
securities, *12*, *13*, *26*, *29*, *70*, *74*, *87*, *105*
securities license, *12*, *13*
security, *62*, *70*, *89*, *96*, *97*
self-insure, *88*
Series 6, *14*, *15*
series 65, *12*, *13*
Series 7, *14*, *15*
shifted the risk, and burden of management, onto the retiree, *97*
shrinking market, *30*
Single Premium Immediate Annuities, *96*
Social Security, 10, 18, 19, 20, 21, 22, 25, *26*, 31, 32, 34, *37*, *38*, *84*, *92*, *118*, 120
Social Security Act of 1934, *25*, *26*
Social Security benefit, *37*

Social Security payroll tax, 38
software programs, *52*
speculating, *62*
SPIA, *97*
spread, *88*, *103*, *147*
spread the risk, *88*
state legal reserve pool, 128
state lotteries, *92*
statistical randomness, *51*
stock brokers, *74*, *80*
stockbrokers, *13*
suitability standard, *14*
suitable advice, *14*
surrender charges, *75*, *82*, *99*, *139*, *140*, *141*, *142*, *144*
Surrender charges, *140*, *141*
surrender periods, *82*, *98*, *99*
surrender terms, *75*
T. Rowe Price, *54*, *109*
Tax, *35*
tax deferral, *26*
Tax deferral, *35*
tax rate, *35*, *36*, *37*, *38*
tax-deferred, *27*
taxes, 10, 19, 21, 27, 35, 36, 37, 38, 84, 118
tax-free accumulation, *36*
tech bubble, *51*
Ted Benna, *23*
Tell Me When You're Going to Die, 1, 2, 4
total market value, 41
traditional annuities, *96*

traditional IRA, *36*
treasuries, 125, 127
Treasury Department, *27*
trillions of dollars vanished, *49*
trust, *8, 13, 14, 16, 83, 145*
trust standard, *13, 14*
trustworthy, *16*
Twin Towers, *51*
U.S. Department of Commerce, 131
U.S. government, *49*
Ulpianus, *24*
uncertainty of lifespan, 10
UPSIDE RISK, 85
VA, *75, 80, 81, 110*
variable annuities, *143, 147*
variable annuity, *2, 74, 75, 80, 81, 83*
VAs, *96, 100, 110*
VIX, *48*

volatility, *48*
Volatility Index, *48*
walk away balance, *110, 111, 112*
Wall Street, *12, 28, 29, 39, 47, 49, 50, 53, 64, 85, 86, 87, 88, 89, 93, 95, 101*
Warren Buffett, *44*
when are you going to die, 9, 52, 59, 89
when are you going to die thing, 52, 59
Wirehouses Warming to Indexed Annuities, *86*
withdrawal rate, *56*
withdrawals, *77, 110, 111*
workers, 24, 25, 29
Xerox, *27, 28*
Your Father's Annuities, *96*

Made in the USA
Middletown, DE
10 April 2017